# NEW CONNECTION
### CEFR B1-B2

Teruhiko Kadoyama
Melanie Scooter
Courtney Hall

BOOK 3

SEIBIDO

**photographs**

iStockphoto

---

**音声ファイルのダウンロード／ストリーミング**

CD マーク表示がある箇所は、音声を弊社 HP より無料でダウンロード／ストリーミングすることができます。トップページのバナーをクリックし、書籍検索してください。書籍詳細ページに音声ダウンロードアイコンがございますのでそちらから自習用音声としてご活用ください。

https://www.seibido.co.jp

---

### New Connection Book 3

Copyright © 2018 LiveABC Interactive Corporation
Japanese edition copyright © Seibido Publishing Co., LTD, Japanese edition
All rights reserved.

*All rights reserved for Japan.*
*No part of this book may be reproduced in any form*
*without permission from Seibido Co., Ltd.*

# CONTENTS

|  | Content Chart | 4 |
|---|---|---|
|  | Learning Overview | 6 |
|  | Introduction | 8 |
| UNIT 1 | Small Talk | 9 |
| UNIT 2 | Reading for Fun | 19 |
| UNIT 3 | Dreams and Ambitions | 29 |
| UNIT 4 | Amazing Inventions | 39 |
| UNIT 5 | The World of Food | 49 |
| UNIT 6 | Art and Creativity | 59 |
| UNIT 7 | Going for Gold | 69 |
| UNIT 8 | Mysteries of the Human Body | 79 |
| UNIT 9 | Architectural Wonders | 89 |
| UNIT 10 | Loving the Earth | 99 |
| UNIT 11 | Expressing Yourself | 109 |
| UNIT 12 | Trends and Fads | 119 |
| UNIT 13 | Seeing the World | 129 |
| UNIT 14 | Therapy and Wellness | 130 |
|  | **LINGUAPORTA** | 149 |

3

# CONTENT CHART

| Unit | Listening & Speaking | Language Focus | Grammar | Reading | Writing | Page |
|---|---|---|---|---|---|---|
| 1 | Fast Friends | Trying to Remember / Discussing Likes and Dislikes | Future Continuous | Avoid Cross-Cultural Conversation Faux Pas! | The Argumentative Essay | pp. 9-18 |
| 2 | Book Report Blues | Showing Understanding / Exchanging Ideas | Causative | More Than Just a Good Story | Topic Sentences / Supporting Sentences | pp. 19-28 |
| 3 | Finding Your Dream Job | Expressing Certainty / Talking About Opportunities and Disappointments | Future in the Past / Perfect Modals | Young and In Charge! | Introduction Hooks / Conclusion Clinchers | pp. 29-38 |
| 4 | Elevator Misery | Overreacting / Talking About Annoyances | Past Perfect | Where the Inventors Come From | Unity and Coherence | pp. 39-48 |
| 5 | Stress Eating | Talking About Your Appetite / Expressing Anxiety | Conditionals | The Future of Food | Generalizations and Examples | pp. 49-58 |
| 6 | Arts Festivals | Discussing Prices / Describing Amazing and Boring Things | Noun Clauses | Where Have All the Artists Gone? | The Process Analysis Essay | pp. 59-68 |
| 7 | Athletic Genetics | Talking About Natural Talents / Qualifying | Adjective Clauses | The Beauty and Power of Water Ballet | Spice Up Your Sentences | pp. 69-78 |

| Unit | Listening & Speaking | Language Focus | Grammar | Reading | Writing | Page |
|---|---|---|---|---|---|---|
| 8 | Organ Printing | Talking About Work / Discussing Fantasy | Adverb Clauses | Disabilities and Genius | The Descriptive Essay | pp. 79-88 |
| 9 | Emotions and Architecture | Feeling Down / Expressing Stress and Comfort | Cleft Sentences | Who Says Buildings Have to Be Boring? | Add Emphasis to Sentences | pp. 89-98 |
| 10 | Turning Trash into Treasure | Searching Thoroughly / Talking About Experts | Participles / Participial Phrases | Overfishing: The Enemy of Ocean Life | The Classification Essay | pp. 99-108 |
| 11 | The Power of Language | Wasting Time / Studying Something | Indirect Speech | What Did It Say? | Choose the Best Voice | pp. 109-118 |
| 12 | Sensational Cosplay | Talking About Unusual and Common Things / Discussing Fashions | Past Perfect Continuous | Dying to Be Beautiful | The Opinion Essay | pp. 119-128 |
| 13 | When in Rome, Do as the Romans Do | Discussing Being Right and Wrong / Getting into Difficult Situations | Wh-ever Words | Get Rich Quick by Traveling! | The Narrative Essay | pp. 129-138 |
| 14 | Internet Abuse and Addiction | Being Supportive and Unsupportive / Facing the Consequences | Future Perfect Continuous | The Changing Face of Alternative Medicine | Paraphrasing vs. Summarizing | pp. 139-148 |

# LEARNING OVERVIEW

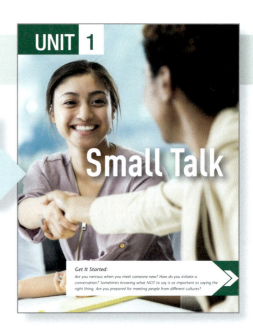

**1 Get It Started**
Introduces discussion questions to break the ice

**2 Vocabulary**
Teaches topic-related vocabulary words

**3 Listening & Speaking**
Presents a real-life dialog

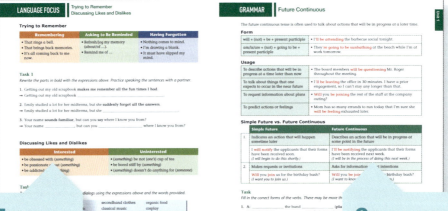

**4 Language Focus**
Expands on useful expressions from Listening & Speaking

**5 Grammar**
Presents a thorough explanation of the main grammar point of the unit

**6 Reading**
Features an interesting article related to the central theme of the unit

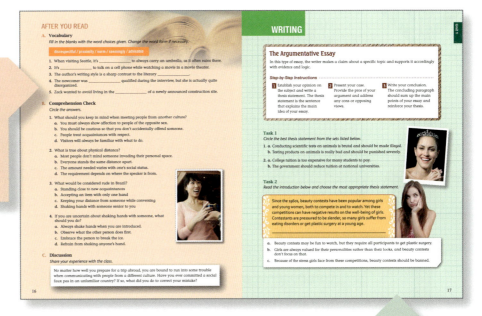

**7 After You Read**
Introduces vocabulary and comprehension exercises based on the content from Reading

**8 Writing**
Teaches writing strategies through step-by-step exercises

**9 Extra Writing Practice**
Provides a writing assignment based on the theme of the unit

7

# INTRODUCTION

Welcome to *New Connection Book 3*. This is the third book in a series created to propel learners towards greater fluency in English. Outstanding English skills are the key to opening doors in today's international world, and no matter how ambitious a student's learning goals may be, the New Connection series will provide the necessary strategies for successful communication.

Each unit of *New Connection Book 3* follows a set structure designed to push students to put what they have learned into practice as well as to challenge them to expand their skills. The unit begins with a Vocabulary section, which utilizes both audio and visual methods to introduce words related to the topic. This is followed by a Listening & Speaking section in which students will have the chance to watch videos of real-life situations. Language Focus and Grammar sections further expand on expressions and grammar concepts presented in the Listening & Speaking section. Both components contain review exercises that help students become accustomed to authentic English.

Students will then move on to Reading, which features a topic-related article accompanied by discussion questions and comprehension tasks. The final section is Writing, which teaches and tests composition techniques. The section comes to a close with a writing assignment based on the theme of the unit.

As students progress through each level, they must utilize the language points they've learned. Students thus become equipped to take on new challenges that will help them achieve English proficiency. Through its well-tested teaching strategies, the *New Connection* series aids students in fulfilling their educational potential.

# UNIT 1

# Small Talk

**Get It Started:**
Are you nervous when you meet someone new? How do you initiate a conversation? Sometimes knowing what NOT to say is as important as saying the right thing. Are you prepared for meeting people from different cultures?

# VOCABULARY

## Task 1
*Match the following words with their correct definitions.*  1-02

1. endeavor _____
2. dependable _____
3. ring a bell _____
4. down in the dumps _____
5. coincidence _____
6. acquaintance _____
7. take a rain check _____

a. reliable
b. depressed
c. the fact of two things happening at the same time by chance
d. to refuse an invitation but say that you might accept it later
e. someone you know, but who is not a close friend
f. to sound familiar
g. an attempt

## Task 2
*Fill in the blanks with the word choices given.*

> get along / awesome / compatible / occupied / colleague

1. The boss and her new assistant are so _____. They work together with ease.
2. My _____ Rhonda is really reliable. She is a great person to work with.
3. Rachel is impossible to _____ with. She acts like she's better than everyone!
4. Mr. Smith is _____ at the moment. Can I take a message?
5. Their last concert was really _____. We enjoyed every minute of it.

# LISTENING & SPEAKING

### A. Comprehension Check

*Listen to the conversation and circle the answers.*  1-03

1. What does Emma think of Vivian when they meet?
   a. Vivian is an old friend of hers.
   b. Vivian is on good terms with Rita.
   c. Vivian isn't an acquaintance of hers.

2. How does Vivian remind Emma of their previous introduction?
   a. She asks Emma about the time she has spent with Rita in Spain.
   b. She claims that they were both present at the same social gathering.
   c. She tells Emma that she bears a close resemblance to Rita.

3. What is Emma and Vivian's shared opinion of Rita?
   a. She is always down in the dumps.
   b. She is always loyal and devoted to her friends.
   c. She ought to be less obsessed with exotic cultures.

4. Why does Vivian feel grateful to Emma?
   a. Her language skills are notably improving.
   b. She is greatly calmed by what Emma says to her.
   c. She has finally found a reliable study partner.

10

**B.** **Partial Dictation**

*Listen again and fill in the blanks.* 1-03

# FAST FRIENDS

*Vivian and Emma are spending a semester abroad. They meet on campus.*

**Vivian:** Hey, aren't you Emma Slattery?

**Emma:** Yes. And you are . . . ?

**Vivian:** Come on! It's not like I'm a complete stranger. I'm Vivian Davis. We have a mutual 1. _____—Rita Skinner.

**Emma:** I'm buddy-buddy with Rita, but could you jog my memory of how we met?

**Vivian:** At her last birthday bash. She's obsessed with Spanish culture, so that was the party's theme. It was a blast!

**Emma:** Oh, that 2. _____ a bell. Yes, I do remember you. What a coincidence. It's nice to see you again.

**Vivian:** Likewise. Have you heard from Rita since you rolled in?

**Emma:** Yeah. She said she's going to be studying abroad for a year as well. She wished me the best and 3. _____ to keep in touch.

**Vivian:** She's such a 4. _____ friend, isn't she?

**Emma:** For sure. It's awesome that I can trust her with my innermost 5. _____. So, have you gotten accustomed to living in Ireland yet?

**Vivian:** Frankly, homesickness has me down in the 6. _____.

**Emma:** Tell me about it. I think I'll truly be missing everyone soon. It helps to remember that this semester will be a worthwhile 7. _____ _____.

**Vivian:** Thanks for the encouragement. Bumping into you has done me a world of good.

**Emma:** Happy to help. I'll be 8. _____ the barbecue social tonight. Do you want to come?

**Vivian:** Sorry. I'll take a rain check. Barbecue socials are not really my cup of tea.

**Emma:** No problem. See you tomorrow.

**buddy-buddy:** very friendly

**bash:** a large party

**blast:** an enjoyable experience

**roll in:** to arrive

**awesome:** very good

**innermost:** deepest

**bump into:** to meet someone by chance

**not someone's cup of tea:** not what someone likes

**Practice the conversation with your partner.**

# LANGUAGE FOCUS
Trying to Remember
Discussing Likes and Dislikes

**Trying to Remember**

| Remembering | Asking to Be Reminded | Having Forgotten |
|---|---|---|
| • That rings a bell.<br>• That brings back memories.<br>• It's all coming back to me now. | • Refresh/jog my memory (about/of . . . ).<br>• Remind me of . . . | • Nothing comes to mind.<br>• I'm drawing a blank.<br>• It must have slipped my mind. |

## Task 1
*Rewrite the parts in bold with the expressions above. Practice speaking the sentences with a partner.*

1. Getting out my old scrapbook **makes me remember all the fun times I had**.
   → Getting out my old scrapbook _____.

2. Emily studied a lot for her midterms, but she **suddenly forgot all the answers**.
   → Emily studied a lot for her midterms, but she _____.

3. Your name **sounds familiar**, but can you **say** where I know you from?
   → Your name _____, but can you _____ where I know you from?

**Discussing Likes and Dislikes**

| Interested | Uninterested |
|---|---|
| • be obsessed with (something)<br>• be passionate about (something)<br>• be addicted to (something) | • (something) be not (one's) cup of tea<br>• be bored stiff by (something)<br>• (something) doesn't do anything for (someone) |

## Task 2
*Pair up with a classmate and create dialogs using the expressions above and the words provided.*

| snorkeling | karaoke | secondhand clothes | organic food |
| boxing | pop music | classical music | cosplay |

*Example*

A: I'm **passionate about** outdoor activities. Maybe I'll take up snorkeling.

B: Really? I'm **bored stiff by** water sports. They're **not my cup of tea**.

# GRAMMAR | Future Continuous

The future continuous tense is often used to talk about actions that will be in progress at a later time.

## Form

| | |
|---|---|
| will + (not) + be + present participle | • I'**ll be attending** the barbecue social tonight. |
| am/is/are + (not) + going to be + present participle | • They'**re going to be sunbathing** at the beach while I'm at work tomorrow. |

## Usage

| | |
|---|---|
| To describe actions that will be in progress at a time later than now | • The board members **will be questioning** Mr. Roger throughout the meeting. |
| To talk about things that one expects to occur in the near future | • I'**ll be leaving** the office in 30 minutes. I have a prior engagement, so I can't stay any longer than that. |
| To request information about plans | • **Will** you **be joining** the rest of the staff at the company outing? |
| To predict actions or feelings | • Mom has so many errands to run today that I'm sure she **will be feeling** exhausted later. |

## Simple Future vs. Future Continuous

| | Simple Future | Future Continuous |
|---|---|---|
| 1. | Indicates an action that will happen sometime later | Describes an action that will be in progress at some point in the future |
| | I **will notify** the applicants that their forms have been received soon. *(I will begin to do this shortly.)* | I'**ll be notifying** the applicants that their forms have been received next week. *(I will be in the process of doing this next week.)* |
| 2. | Makes requests or invitations | Asks for information about intentions |
| | **Will** you **join** us for the birthday bash? *(I want you to join us.)* | **Will** you **be joining** us for the birthday bash? *(I want to know if you plan to join us.)* |

## Task

*Fill in the correct forms of the verbs. There may be more than one possible answer.*

1. A: _____ the band _____ (**play**) when the fireworks display starts?

   B: Yes, but they _____ (**end**) their performance shortly afterwards.

   A: We _____ (**need**) to get there early.

2. A: Next week, Dad _____ (**mingle**) with government officials at the White House.

   B: Yeah. He _____ (**stand**) next to the president when the camera crews show up.

3. A: Mr. Johnson _____ (**not take**) calls until the afternoon.

   B: OK. I _____ (**try**) contacting him again at around 3:00 p.m.

4. A: _____ Claire still _____ (**prepare**) the paperwork when the clients arrive?

   B: I don't think so; I expect that she _____ (**finish**) up ahead of time.

# READING

## BEFORE YOU READ  1-04
*Preview the article below and make predictions.*

1. What does **faux pas** in the title mean?
   a. Embarrassing mistakes
   b. Common ideas
   c. Warm greetings
   d. Awkward topics

2. What do you think the article is mainly about?
   a. Traveling to the most cultural places
   b. How to quickly make friends with local people
   c. How to approach people from other cultures
   d. The best way to shake hands

# Avoid Cross-Cultural Conversation Faux Pas!

1   Traveling in a foreign country can be a total disaster, especially if you are unfamiliar with the social norms. Everything from where you stand to how you move your hands can be insulting. To avoid embarrassing situations, it's helpful to learn some basic etiquette before you head off to your next travel destination.

## Too Close?

When initiating a conversation, note how close you are standing to the person opposite you. Personal space is an essential concept in many cultures, and how much or little you give often affects the first impression you make. For example, in most Western nations, locals do not like standing close to one another. In these countries, it is customary for people to back away when they feel their space has been violated. On the other hand, South Americans stand in close proximity to one another. When you are meeting one of them, keep in mind that it's disrespectful to step backwards during a conversation. A good rule of thumb is to stand at least an arm's length away from your speaking partner.

14

## Shake or Not?

Another thing to consider when greeting someone is whether or not to shake hands. While
20  it is appropriate to do so in some places, in others it will be damaging to your reputation. Take Thailand, for instance. Thai people generally find it unacceptable to make any public physical contact with members of the opposite sex. Conversely, in
25  France, men will often kiss the cheeks of female acquaintances. If you don't know whether or not you should shake hands, it is advisable to wait for the other person to make the first move.

## Which Hand Is Right?

The next question is what you will be doing with your hands during other types of
30  interactions. In Hindu and Islamic cultures, the left hand is regarded as unclean; therefore, you should never shake hands or pass things to people with your left hand. In Asia, it is important to use both hands when giving and accepting items; otherwise, you'll appear careless and impolite.

Seemingly simple encounters can actually be quite complicated. Be aware of what is
35  considered courteous in other cultures. Doing a little research in advance can ensure that your cross-cultural experiences are rewarding instead of embarrassing.

# AFTER YOU READ

## A. Vocabulary

*Fill in the blanks with the word choices given. Change the word form if necessary.*

> **disrespectful / proximity / norm / seemingly / advisable**

1. When visiting Seattle, it's _____ to always carry an umbrella, as it often rains there.

2. It's _____ to talk on a cell phone while watching a movie in a movie theater.

3. The author's writing style is a sharp contrast to the literary _____.

4. The newcomer was _____ qualified during the interview, but she is actually quite disorganized.

5. Zack wanted to avoid living in the _____ of a newly announced construction site.

## B. Comprehension Check

*Circle the answers.*

1. What should you keep in mind when meeting people from another culture?
   a. You must always show affection to people of the opposite sex.
   b. You should be cautious so that you don't accidentally offend someone.
   c. People treat acquaintances with respect.
   d. Visitors will always be familiar with what to do.

2. What is true about physical distance?
   a. Most people don't mind someone invading their personal space.
   b. Everyone stands the same distance apart.
   c. The amount needed varies with one's social status.
   d. The requirement depends on where the speaker is from.

3. What would be considered rude in Brazil?
   a. Standing close to new acquaintances
   b. Accepting an item with only one hand
   c. Keeping your distance from someone while conversing
   d. Shaking hands with someone senior to you

4. If you are uncertain about shaking hands with someone, what should you do?
   a. Always shake hands when you are introduced.
   b. Observe what the other person does first.
   c. Embrace the person to break the ice.
   d. Refrain from shaking anyone's hand.

## C. Discussion

*Share your experience with the class.*

No matter how well you prepare for a trip abroad, you are bound to run into some trouble when communicating with people from a different culture. Have you ever committed a social faux pas in an unfamiliar country? If so, what did you do to correct your mistake?

# WRITING

## The Argumentative Essay

In this type of essay, the writer makes a claim about a specific topic and supports it accordingly with evidence and logic.

### Step-by-Step Instructions

**1** Establish your opinion on the subject and write a thesis statement. The thesis statement is the sentence that explains the main idea of your essay.

**2** Present your case. Provide the pros of your argument and address any cons or opposing views.

**3** Write your conclusion. The concluding paragraph should sum up the main points of your essay and reinforce your thesis.

### Task 1
Circle the best thesis statement from the sets listed below.

1. a. Conducting scientific tests on animals is brutal and should be made illegal.
   b. Testing products on animals is really bad and should be punished severely.

2. a. College tuition is too expensive for many students to pay.
   b. The government should reduce tuition at national universities.

### Task 2
Read the introduction below and choose the most appropriate thesis statement.

Since the 1960s, beauty contests have been popular among girls and young women, both to compete in and to watch. Yet these competitions can have negative results on the well-being of girls. Contestants are pressured to be slender, so many girls suffer from eating disorders or get plastic surgery at a young age.
_____

a. Beauty contests may be fun to watch, but they require all participants to get plastic surgery.
b. Girls are always valued for their personalities rather than their looks, and beauty contests don't focus on that.
c. Because of the stress girls face from these competitions, beauty contests should be banned.

# EXTRA WRITING PRACTICE

## BEFORE YOU WRITE
*What's your viewpoint on Internet relationships? Organize the following points into the chart below.*

a. Easily disguise identity
b. Make friendships and meet dates
c. Comfortably introduce oneself to total strangers
d. Share photos and favorite websites
e. Not have the opportunity to meet an Internet acquaintance face-to-face
f. Make children an easy target for Internet criminals

Add your own ideas

| Pros | Cons |
| --- | --- |
|  |  |

## WRITE IT UP
*Write an argumentative essay arguing FOR Internet relationships. Follow the prompts on the left.*

### The Internet: Connecting Our Lives

**Introduction:** Write a thesis statement.
→ With modern technology, online relationships are becoming more and more common. Facebook, Twitter, chat rooms, and blog sites are all useful tools for establishing relations over the Internet.

**Pros:** List two or three supporting reasons.
→ Like it or not, society will only be relying more on Internet resources as technology progresses.

**Cons:** Address the opposing view.
→ Those against Internet relationships typically oppose them because of safety concerns.

**Conclusion:** Summarize your position.
→ Once you think about it, the web really isn't a scary place to meet new people.

# VOCABULARY

### Task 1
*Match the following words with their correct definitions.*  1-05

1. tedious _____
2. disciplined _____
3. deprive _____
4. swamp _____
5. thought-provoking _____
6. suspend _____
7. stressed-out _____

a. stimulating
b. behaving in a very controlled way
c. to make someone leave their school for a short time
d. to take something away from someone
e. too anxious and tired to be able to relax
f. boring
g. to suddenly give someone a lot of work to deal with

### Task 2
*Fill in the blanks with the word choices given. Change the word form if necessary.*

| biography / earnestly / description / terrifying / leisure |
|---|

1. A horror novel tells a _____ story about ghosts or killers.
2. The article was criticized because it depicted Asian people negatively. Many of its _____ were offensive.
3. A _____ is non-fiction. It includes actual events that occur in someone's life.
4. Reading for recreation is a great _____ activity that can actually increase one's intelligence.
5. To further immerse herself in studying the early 19th century, Cheryl _____ read novels set during that time period.

# LISTENING & SPEAKING

### A. Comprehension Check
*Listen to the conversation and check **T** if the statement is true, **F** if it's false.*  1-06

1. T ☐ F ☐ Both of the students are working under intense pressure to meet the deadline for the upcoming book report.
2. T ☐ F ☐ Phil suggests that Tony read the biography of a famous surfer.
3. T ☐ F ☐ Phil points out how serious the consequences of cheating are.
4. T ☐ F ☐ Tony initially expected that the assignment would require little effort.
5. T ☐ F ☐ Tony regularly tries to engage in his studies.

B. **Partial Dictation**

Listen again and fill in the blanks.  1-06

# Book Report Blues

Phil tries to inspire Tony to get his book report done.

**Tony:** I need to have my head examined. I think I'm going insane!

**Phil:** What's up?

**Tony:** I'm 1. _____ about the book report due next week. And reading is so tedious.

**Phil:** Do you understand what the teacher is looking for?

**Tony:** It beats me. Can I pick your brain for some ideas? Maybe we can brainstorm tonight.

**Phil:** Sorry, dude. I have a doctor's appointment.

**Tony:** You've really been 2. _____ lately, huh?

**Phil:** Unfortunately, yes. I haven't had any time for extracurricular 3. _____. Wait. I just had an idea! You have an obsession with surfing, so why don't you read the biography of a renowned surfer?

**Tony:** That might be good for recreational reading, but it wouldn't be 4. _____ enough for a book report. I'm totally stuck. I'm thinking of having my report written by a friend instead of going through all this trouble.

**Phil:** If you cheat, you'll deprive yourself of an opportunity to learn, and you'll also risk getting 5. _____.

**Tony:** OK, OK. I get the picture. I was just messing around. But this report is 6. _____ my imagination. I thought writing it would be as easy as pie.

**Phil:** Well, if you put your mind to it, I'm sure you'll pass with flying colors.

**Tony:** I guess you're right. I need to be more 7. _____ and stop putting it off.

**Phil:** You 8. _____ regret putting in the extra effort. Good luck!

*Practice the conversation with your partner.*

---

**insane:** crazy

**brainstorm:** to have a discussion for solving a problem

**obsession:** something that you think about all the time

**mess around:** to behave in a silly way
**as easy as pie:** very easy

**with flying colors:** very well

21

## LANGUAGE FOCUS: Showing Understanding / Exchanging Ideas

### Showing Understanding

| Understanding Something | Not Understanding Something |
|---|---|
| • get the picture<br>• hear (*someone*) loud and clear<br>• have got it | • (it) beats me<br>• you've got me<br>• be at a loss |

### Task 1

Listen and decide if Olivia knows about the things listed. Write the suggestions she gives.  🎧 1-07

| | Ideas | Does She Know? | Suggestions |
|---|---|---|---|
| 1 | What a Phillips-head screwdriver is | | |
| 2 | How to begin the assembly process | | |
| 3 | How to move the heavy bars | | |
| 4 | Who could complete the assembly | | |

### Exchanging Ideas

| Asking for Opinions | Brainstorming |
|---|---|
| • pick (*one's*) brain<br>• get (*one's*) input/view on (*something*)<br>• bounce (*something*) off (*someone*) | • put our heads together<br>• rack (*one's*) brain<br>• kick around some ideas |

### Task 2

Act out the situations with a partner using the expressions above.

> 1. You've been assigned a chemistry project.
> 2. Your friend is writing an article about famine in Africa.
> 3. You're getting ready for a presentation on global warming.

*Example*

A: Can I **get your input on** this assignment? I think it's going to be a tough one.

B: I'm sure if we **put our heads together**, we will think up something spectacular.

# GRAMMAR | Causative

Causative verbs are used to show that a person or thing makes something else happen. These verbs can be used in any tense.

## Structure

| Active Causative |
| --- |
| have + someone/something + V |
| • We'll **have** the doctor **prescribe** you some medicine. |
| get + someone/something + to V |
| • Can you **get** the accountant **to tackle** this problem? |
| make + someone/something + V |
| • The teacher will **make** you **stay** after class if you don't hand in your paper promptly. |
| let + someone/something + V |
| • The manager will **let** you **take** annual leave after the first year of employment. |

| Passive Causative |
| --- |
| have + someone/something + past participle |
| • I need to **have** my head **examined**. |
| get + someone/something + past participle |
| • Cheating on the test will **get** you **suspended**. |

**Usage Note**

Other causative verbs include allow, convince, employ, encourage, permit, and require. These verbs are followed by **to V**.

**Example:**
• The professor encouraged his students to apply for the scholarship.

## Difference between *Have* and *Get*

| Use *Have* or *Get* | |
| --- | --- |
| In imperatives | • **Have** the supplies **delivered** to the company's address.<br>• **Get** this layout **finished** before the presentation. |
| **Often Use *Get*** | |
| For successfully persuading someone to do something | • Sheila **got** her roommate **to edit** her proposal before she submitted it. |
| **Often Use *Have*** | |
| For paying someone to have something done | • Mr. Sullivan **had** the barber **trim** his mustache. |

## Task

*Rewrite the following sentences using the correct forms of the causative verbs provided.*

1. Ryan wanted the gardener to landscape the yard before the barbecue was held. (**have**)

   _____

2. Nancy pleaded with the Hardy brothers to help her solve the mystery before it was too late. (**get**)

   _____

3. Felix intends to submit his application three weeks prior to the deadline. (**get**)

   _____

4. Louise crashed the car because she was texting, so her parents took away her cell phone. (**have**)

   _____

23

# READING

# MORE THAN JUST A GOOD STORY

1   To many, reading seems like a tiresome pursuit. While books are commonly credited with broadening people's knowledge, some people don't enjoy reading because it reminds them of schoolwork. However, reading doesn't have to be tedious. Besides providing pleasure, it is a great way to relieve physical and mental tension.

5   The expression "curl up with a good book" perfectly illustrates the refreshment that reading can provide. Studies have shown that it's the most effective means of achieving relaxation, outdoing more standard practices. In tested subjects, listening to music reduced stress levels by 61 percent, sipping a cup of tea by 54 percent, and taking a walk by 42 percent. Reading's effects are much
10   greater, decreasing anxiety by 68 percent! In fact, those tested only needed six minutes of reading to cut mental pressure by more than two thirds.

Psychologists believe that the act of
15   entering into a story is so distracting that it eases muscle tightness. So, if a fictional world is the calming factor, shouldn't TV accomplish the same results? It does, but not as well. People often turn to TV programs
20   when they want to relax. The average

### BEFORE YOU READ  1-08

*After a busy day, what's your favorite way to relax? Number the choices below according to your preferences. Compare your answers with a classmate's.*

☐ Listening to some soothing music ☐ Enjoying a cup of hot tea
☐ Taking a stroll around town ☐ Reading for recreation

*Skim the article to discover which action is the most relaxing based on the latest research findings. Are you surprised?*

American adult spends as much as 15 years of his or her life watching TV. But reading is a more soothing form of escape because it demands the reader's utmost attention. A story absorbs the brain with the presented information and diverts one's mind from worries. In contrast, the minimal concentration needed by a television program still allows the mind to wander and focus on other things.

Reading produces an effect on the brain similar to that of meditation. According to researchers, when students read silently, they read four to seven words per second. Scientists determined decades ago that seeing four to seven flashes of light per second transports the brain into the Theta rhythm—the same phase in which meditation occurs. This is the condition of maximum concentration, and the brain blocks out all interruptions. Therefore, when the brain is reading, it is actually in an altered state of consciousness.

The next time you come home exhausted and reach for the remote, do your brain a favor and immerse yourself in a story instead.

# AFTER YOU READ

### A. Vocabulary

*Fill in the blanks with the word choices given. Change the word form if necessary.*

> **comfort / expand / surpass / awareness / modified**

1. Lullabies are soothing to infants. They are often sung before bedtime because they are such a(n) _____.

2. The members of the sales team want to _____ each other, as they've been told that whoever outdoes the others will receive additional vacation days.

3. The research project broadened the students' knowledge of psychology. They all agreed that the exercise had _____ their understanding.

4. The illness is the result of a(n) _____ version of the virus. The altered virus doesn't respond to the usual treatment.

5. One of the first effects of being deprived of oxygen is a loss of consciousness. Once a person has lost _____, his or her chances of survival are low.

### B. Comprehension Check

*Answer the questions.*

1. According to the writer, why isn't everyone interested in reading?

2. In what way is reading capable of relieving one's mind of stress?

3. What is the reason that watching television is not as relaxing as reading?

4. How does the condition of one's brain change while reading?

### C. Discussion

*Share your opinion with the class.*

Studies have shown that . . .

1. reading is the best activity to do directly prior to bedtime.
2. readers are three times as likely as those who do not read to participate in charity work.
3. readers are usually passionate about traveling.

Why do you think this is ?

# WRITING

## Topic Sentences

A **topic sentence** presents the main point of a paragraph.
To write a topic sentence:

|  | Key Point | Example |
|---|---|---|
| Step 1 | Choose the topic of your paragraph. | reading |
| Step 2 | Select a main idea about the topic. | Reading is a hobby. |
| Step 3 | Narrow the main idea into a controlling idea. A controlling idea is a specific concept that you want to explain about the topic. | Reading is a constructive hobby because it expands readers' vocabulary. |

## Supporting Sentences

Supporting sentences develop the main point of the paragraph.
The support can be: ☑details ☑facts ☑examples ☑quotations ☑explanations

## Task 1

*Finish the topic sentence by circling the best controlling idea.*

**1** Dogs are a popular pet choice . . .
   a. because of their loyal and affectionate nature.
   b. , and they bark aggressively, too.

**2** When I was a child, my grandmother's cookies . . .
   a. were usually chocolate chunk.
   b. always made me cheerful.

**3** Patrick Dempsey's dark hair . . .
   a. makes him the best-looking American actor.
   b. often hangs in his eyes.

**4** Students strive to avoid poor grades . . .
   a. by studying with diligence.
   b. and disappointing their parents.

## Task 2

*Read the paragraph below. Then write an improved topic sentence.*

**E-readers are nice to have.** With electronic reading devices, such as Amazon's Kindle and Barnes & Noble's Nook, eager readers can download online versions of their favorite titles. Now, instead of dragging around multiple heavy books, readers can simply pack a light e-reader to take hundreds of stories with them wherever they go. They take the hassle out of reading on the go.

**Improved Topic Sentence:**

_____

_____

# EXTRA WRITING PRACTICE

## BEFORE YOU WRITE
*Write the letter of each description underneath the author it best describes.*

a. Best-selling author of horror and suspense novels

b. Classical novelist of the 1800s

c. Fantasy series demonstrates an amazing imagination

d. Was inspired during a train ride from Manchester to London in 1990

e. Wrote highly acclaimed English literature that is still studied today

f. Work has sold over 350 million copies and been adapted into several scary films

g. Must-read titles include *A Tale of Two Cities* and *Oliver Twist*

h. Has enthusiastic adult and child fans

i. Has been terrifying audiences since the 1970s

## WRITE IT UP
Choose one of the above authors and describe why you admire him or her. Use phrases and vocabulary from the previous section in your passage. You can write about your favorite author if you are not familiar with any of these authors.

**Answer these questions in your passage.**

1. How many books have you read by this author?
2. What was your reaction the first time you read his or her work?
3. What would you say to the author if you met face-to-face?

### The Writer I Admire Most

# UNIT 3

# Dreams and Ambitions

### Get It Started:
Walt Disney once said, "If you can dream it, you can do it." What is your dream?
Do you want to be a doctor, a politician, or maybe even an actor?
Do your friends and family support your dreams and goals?

# VOCABULARY

## Task 1
Match the following words with their correct definitions.

1. down-to-earth ____
2. aptitude ____
3. enormous ____
4. relate ____
5. surgeon ____
6. yearn ____
7. aspiration ____

a. ambition
b. natural ability
c. to have a strong desire for something
d. very large
e. practical
f. to feel that you understand someone's problem, situation, etc.
g. a doctor who does operations in a hospital

## Task 2
Take the quiz. Then use the chart on the right to determine your personality type. After that, listen to the audio and decide what kind of personality type Lucy has.

**1. At school, you have to follow a rigid schedule. This makes you feel:**
- Ⓐ **annoyed.** You like to work at your own pace.
- Ⓑ **bothered.** You have a party to go to!
- Ⓒ **relaxed.** You feel at ease when there's a plan.

**2. In basketball, you like:**
- Ⓐ **trying different positions.** You can help your team from anywhere on the floor!
- Ⓑ **playing the shooting guard.** You get excited by scoring points.
- Ⓒ **being a cheerleader.** You love cheering on the home team.

**3. You flunked a test. Your response is to:**
- Ⓐ **study harder.** You are confident that you can improve.
- Ⓑ **blow it off.** It's just a little test after all.
- Ⓒ **feel guilty.** You disappointed your parents.

### What's your type?

If you answered mostly A, you are a **go-getter.** You are motivated to accomplish big goals. You are competitive, but you can also be flexible. You'd make an ideal entrepreneur.

If you answered mostly B, you are a **socializer.** You are energetic and love being in the spotlight. You have a fun personality and the potential to be an exceptional salesperson.

If you answered mostly C, you are a **duty-fulfiller.** You stick to rules and dislike taking risks. Loyalty and dependability are your best qualities. Being a clerk could be a good fit.

*Don't worry if you have different answers. Everyone is a unique blend!*

**What's Lucy's type?**

go-getter / socializer / duty-fulfiller

# LISTENING & SPEAKING

## A. Comprehension Check
Listen to the conversation and check **T** if the statement is true, **F** if it's false.

1. T☐ F☐ Tina hasn't come to a conclusion concerning her career path.
2. T☐ F☐ Tina's mother used to work as an ER nurse.
3. T☐ F☐ Jimmy is confident of becoming a successful comedian.
4. T☐ F☐ Jimmy's parents recommend that he go into book sales.
5. T☐ F☐ Tina hopes to do some intellectual job in the future.

B. **Partial Dictation**

Listen again and fill in the blanks.  1-11

# Finding Your Dream Job

*Jimmy and Tina discuss their future careers.*

**Jimmy:** Hey, Tina. Have you made any plans for after graduation?

**Tina:** I was planning to be a 1. _____, but nothing is set in stone.

**Jimmy:** That's a good fit for you since you find it satisfying to help others with their discomfort.

**Tina:** Yeah, but my hopes were dashed when I saw the 2. _____ tuition costs. I'm not interested in being in debt forever, but I also don't want to turn out like my mom. She was going to be an ER nurse and ended up as a housewife.

**Jimmy:** I can relate. You feel like the sky is the limit when you're young, but you have to be down-to-earth when you're an adult. My 3. _____ has always been to become a comedian, but now I'm concerned I'll fall flat on my face.

**Tina:** You tell some hysterical 4. _____. If you are passionate about comedy, you should just go all out!

**Jimmy:** I'm kind of on the fence. My uncle 5. _____ that I go into book sales instead. I adore books, but I don't possess an aptitude for sales. Is being a surgeon really your dream job?

**Tina:** No. In fact, I 6. _____ to do something academic and intellectual. I should have enrolled in that career workshop to get inspiration.

**Jimmy:** I would have 7. _____ up for that, but it was 8. _____ during the same time slot as basketball practice.

**Tina:** Let's go to it together next semester.

**be set in stone:** to be difficult to change

**dash:** to destroy

**ER:** = emergency room

**fall flat on one's face:** to fail completely

**hysterical:** very funny

**on the fence:** not able to decide something

> Practice the conversation with your partner.

# LANGUAGE FOCUS
### Expressing Certainty
### Talking About Opportunities and Disappointments

**Expressing Certainty**

| Certain | Uncertain |
|---|---|
| • (*something*) be set in stone | • (*someone*) be on the fence |
| • (*something*) be a done deal | • (*something*) be up in the air |
| • (*something*) be nailed down | • (*something*) be a toss-up |

## Task 1

*Rewrite the sentences in bold with the expressions above.*

1. **A:** Have you decided which dress you want to purchase for the party?
   **B:** I bought the red one yesterday, so **my decision has been made**.
   → I bought the red one yesterday, so _____.

2. **A:** What has been confirmed for the banquet next week?
   **B:** It beats me. The plans are still **not settled**.
   → It beats me. The plans are still _____.

## Task 2

*Listen to the audio. Check **T** if the statement is true, **F** if it's false.*  1-12

1. T ☐  F ☐   This year's company outing will be held at the Grand Canyon.
2. T ☐  F ☐   Heather prefers accommodations that have a high level of comfort.
3. T ☐  F ☐   The employees will need to make arrangements for sightseeing activities.
4. T ☐  F ☐   The company has decided on how much they can spend on transportation.

**Talking About Opportunities and Disappointments**

| Hopeful | Disappointed |
|---|---|
| • the sky is the limit | • (*one's*) hopes are dashed |
| • the world is (*one's*) oyster | • get/have a reality check |
| • have a rosy future | • be let down (by . . .) |

## Task 3

*Fill in the expressions that fit best.*

1. My parents are always encouraging me to follow my dreams.
   They reassure me _____.

2. I was extremely _____ when I learned that I wasn't accepted for the internship.

# GRAMMAR | Future in the Past / Perfect Modals

## Future in the Past

We normally use the future in the past to talk about something we thought was going to happen. Remember that it is not important whether or not it does actually happen.

| Form | Usage | Example |
|---|---|---|
| would + V | to offer or promise, to predict something | • He promised he **would drive** me to the airport. |
| was/were going to + V | to plan or predict something | • She **was going to be** an ER nurse and ended up as a housewife. |
| was/were + V-ing | to talk about a future situation in the past | • I **was planning** to be a surgeon, but the enormous tuition costs dashed my hopes. |
| was/were + about to + V | to explain that something almost happens when something else happens | • They stopped by my house just as I **was about to leave** for work. |

## Perfect Modals

We often use the following structure to express the degree of certainty about past events: **modal + have + past participle**.

| Perfect Modal | Usage | Example |
|---|---|---|
| **must have + past participle** | fairly certain something happened | • Ted didn't look well this morning. He **must have caught** a cold. |
| **may/might/could have + past participle** | not certain if something happened | • Eddie hasn't gotten here yet. He **may/might/could have missed** the train. |
| **should have + past participle** | needed to do something but did not | • I **should have enrolled in** that career workshop to get inspiration. |
| **would have + past participle** | planned to do something but did not | • I **would have signed** up for that, but I had basketball practice. |

## Task

*Complete the sentences with the choices in the box.*

| | | |
|---|---|---|
| must have assumed | may have finished | might have come |
| could have helped | should have bought | would have passed |

1. I think she _____ a more spacious car. Her family won't fit comfortably in this one.

2. Dad _____ that we were throwing him a surprise party because he didn't look shocked.

3. Shelly admitted that she _____ if I had recruited her to work on the project.

4. Danny _____ the entire bag of cookies. That is why he looks quite ill now.

5. You _____ in first, but you didn't stick to a rigid training schedule throughout the year.

6. The students never _____ the exam without attending the study sessions the previous week.

33

# READING

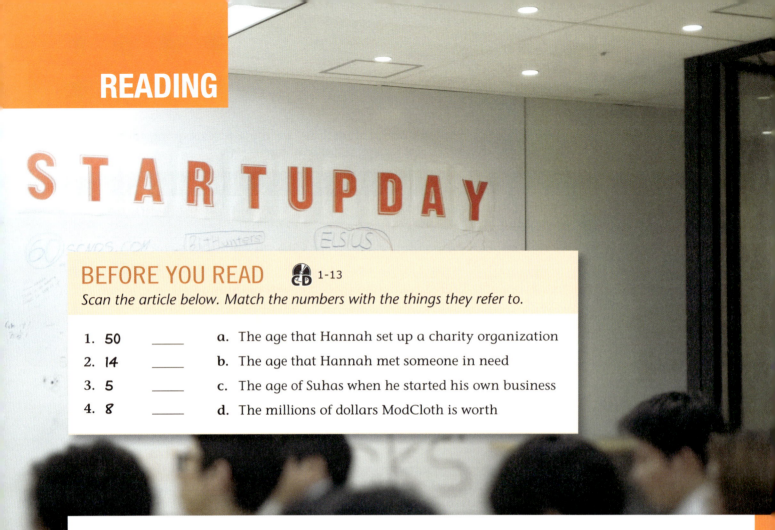

## BEFORE YOU READ  🎧 1-13

Scan the article below. Match the numbers with the things they refer to.

1. 50  \_\_\_\_   a. The age that Hannah set up a charity organization
2. 14  \_\_\_\_   b. The age that Hannah met someone in need
3. 5   \_\_\_\_   c. The age of Suhas when he started his own business
4. 8   \_\_\_\_   d. The millions of dollars ModCloth is worth

# Young and In Charge!

1. It may come as a surprise, but many of the world's leading businesses were established by people under the age of 30. Google, Facebook, and Microsoft, among others, were all set up by college students, and today these companies dominate their respective industries. For those of you who have the makings of a young entrepreneur, read on for inspiration.

5    Susan Gregg Koger has always had a passion for unique clothes and good deals. As a college freshman, she and her boyfriend sold vintage clothing they found at thrift stores through an online shop they created. Although the site was useful for extra income, they knew that if this hobby was going to be a full-time job, they would have to expand. They began purchasing clothing from independent designers to carry along with their vintage
10   findings. Today, ModCloth has over 200 employees, and the company is valued at more than $50 million!

    After teaching himself the ins and outs of programming software and building websites, Suhas Gopinath opened his IT consultancy company, Globals Inc., at the age of 14. Using his shrewd business sense, Suhas
15 registered his business as a corporation and thus became the world's youngest CEO. Now, Globals Inc. has offices in several countries and employs more than 400 people. Even though he could have sold the company for hundreds of millions of dollars, Suhas prefers to continue leading his own enterprise.

20     At five years old, Hannah Taylor saw her first homeless person. She was strongly affected by the realization that some people have nothing and decided that she would assist the needy people of Canada. When she turned eight years old, she founded the Ladybug Foundation. This charity collects funds to help the homeless and raises awareness of the issue. Even though she's now a busy teenager, Hannah still works relentlessly with the
25 foundation. She constantly visits schools and other venues to spread the message that the problem of homelessness could be eliminated.

    Nowadays, young competent and successful business leaders are common all around the world. This shows that no matter your age, when you have the zeal to make your dream a reality, you can launch an organization that will thrive!

35

# AFTER YOU READ

## A. Vocabulary

*Fill in the blanks with the word choices given. Change the word form if necessary.*

> relentlessly / respective / shrewd / eliminate / zeal

1. Samantha showed great _____ for political and social reforms.

2. He worked _____ to finish the project ahead of the deadline.

3. In times of economic recession, the ability to be _____ in business transactions is crucial.

4. Hannah helps raise consciousness about the efforts to _____ homelessness.

5. After the police arrived at the demonstration, the college students retreated to their _____ dorm rooms.

## B. Comprehension Check

*Circle the answers.*

1. Where did Koger find the clothing that she originally sold at ModCloth?

    a. It was made by college students.

    b. It was found at secondhand shops.

    c. It was from her favorite clothing sites.

    d. It was created by self-employed designers.

2. Why has Gopinath NOT sold his company?

    a. He would rather manage it himself.

    b. He hasn't received a worthwhile offer.

    c. He wanted to become the world's youngest CEO.

    d. Investors are reluctant to spend money on such a new venture.

3. What is the objective of Taylor's charity?

    a. To help children who are unaware that homelessness exists

    b. To give advice on how charities can assist a corporation

    c. To tackle the problem of people not having a place to live

    d. To teach people how to sell merchandise online

4. What is true about young entrepreneurs?

    a. They are normally too inefficient to launch their own businesses.

    b. Those under 30 will need abundant financial aid to get started.

    c. Most of them create charities in order to earn recognition.

    d. They have proven to be just as remarkable as older ones.

## C. Discussion

*Share your opinion with the class.*

> Young people who take on huge responsibilities, like a business, can miss out on enjoying youthful freedoms. Look at Mark Zuckerberg, founder of Facebook, or Justin Bieber, pop star. They've made millions but are constantly working to meet people's expectations. What are the advantages and disadvantages of starting a business before adulthood?

# WRITING

## Introduction Hooks

To grab your audience's attention, use a **hook**! It can be:
- ✓ a surprising fact
- ✓ an interesting story
- ✓ a famous quote
- ✓ a rhetorical question

### Task 1
*Write the letter of the hook that best fits the following introductory paragraph.*

_____ Then be an entrepreneur and become your own boss! While turning a profit might be a prolonged process, the positives of working for yourself outnumber the negatives. Everyone has a specialty or skill to offer society. Once you determine what yours is, you'll be on the road to financial freedom.

a. I'd always dreamed of starting a security company, but the uncertainty of generating enough income held me back.

b. Nolan Bushnell, who's founded over 20 successful businesses, once said, "The true entrepreneur is a doer, not a dreamer.".

c. Do you wish you could set your own work schedule? Are you tired of meeting someone else's demands?

d. Even though large corporations dominate the US economy, small businesses employ roughly 50 percent of America's workers.

## Conclusion Clinchers

A **clincher** is the conclusion's impacting final statement. An effective clincher refers back to the hook by:
- ✓ making a prediction based on the fact
- ✓ finishing the story
- ✓ mentioning the quotation
- ✓ asking a final rhetorical question

### Task 2
*Write a conclusion clincher below. Relate it to the hook you chose in Task 1.*

Having a flexible schedule, choosing your colleagues, and feeling fulfilled by your work are all motivating reasons to become self-employed. _____
_____
_____

# EXTRA WRITING PRACTICE

## BEFORE YOU WRITE

*Visit the site www.thehersheycompany.com to learn about The Hershey Company. Write down information that could be used as a hook and/or clincher in an essay about the company.*

|  STATISTICS |  STORIES |  SAYINGS |
|---|---|---|
| • Hershey's employs around 13,700 employees and sells $4 billion worth of products annually. | • | • "Caramels are only a fad. Chocolate is a permanent thing." — Milton Hershey |

## WRITE IT UP

*Write an introduction and conclusion for the essay about Hershey's below. Use the information you collected above to write an effective hook and clincher.*

**Title:** _____ (Be creative.)

_____
_____
_____
_____

    Milton Hershey was born in rural Pennsylvania in 1857. Despite growing up with little formal education, Milton established the successful Lancaster Caramel Company. He became passionate about the art of making chocolate and began coating his caramel candies in it. Chocolate was expensive back then, and Milton realized that he could find a way to manufacture affordable chocolate so that everyone would be able to enjoy its rich taste. After numerous experiments, he discovered a recipe for delicious milk chocolate. Hershey's chocolate was born!

    The Hershey's chocolate bar was quite profitable, and Milton put those profits to good use. He believed that workers who were treated well would produce better products. Therefore, he made improving his town a priority, spending money to build a community building, convention hall, and schools. In fact, Milton Hershey School has been providing education to children from lower-income families since 1909. Hershey, PA, could have been a completely different place if it weren't for Milton's charity.

_____
_____
_____
_____

# UNIT 4

# Amazing Inventions

**Get It Started:**
*Do you have any thoughts on how to make the world a better place? The things we normally take for granted in the modern world, like computers, lightbulbs, or air-conditioning, were once just concepts in some people's minds. What ideas are in your mind?*

# VOCABULARY

## Task 1

*Match the following words with their correct definitions.* 🎧 1-14

1. nag _____
2. trigger _____
3. exhausted _____
4. annoyance _____
5. ingenious _____
6. install _____
7. backbreaking _____

a. something that makes you slightly angry
b. to fix a piece of equipment into position so that it can be used
c. very hard and tiring
d. to keep asking someone to do something
e. very tired
f. extremely creative
g. to cause

## Task 2

*Look at the following chindōgu inventions. Fill in the blanks with the words from the box below.*

chores / creativity / feasible / patented / prototype / utility

### Dog Wigs

Although this invention may never be
1. _____ by any country, the dog
wig 2. _____ has started a new
trend in puppy fashion. These colorful wigs
come in almost any shape
imaginable and are a very
3. _____ style option
for your beloved pet!

### The Baby Mop

Using some 4. _____, parents
can get their infants to help with
5. _____ while they crawl.
Though most baby clothes have little or no
6. _____, The Baby
Mop assists with housecleaning
during the course of normal
activities!

# LISTENING & SPEAKING

## A. Comprehension Check

*Listen to the conversation and circle the answers.* 🎧 1-15

1. What exaggeration does Bradley make?
   a. Taking the stairs might result in a heart attack.
   b. He has difficulty breathing because he ran up four flights of stairs.
   c. Nagging is an effective way to get help from someone.

2. What is Courtney's opinion about laziness?
   a. Lazy people would never walk up a flight of stairs.
   b. Laziness can be a motivator for inventiveness.
   c. Laziness cannot be attributed to inventions.

3. What is true about the first passenger elevator?
   a. Otis's sons constructed it according to their father's plans.
   b. Modern elevators adopted its brake system design.
   c. The device was invented for one particular person.

4. Why does Bradley want to become an elevator engineer?
   a. He would be able to secure a high income in that profession.
   b. He would be assured of always having an elevator to ride.
   c. He would like to copy the Otis business model.

B. **Partial Dictation**

Listen again and fill in the blanks. 🎧 1-15

# ELEVATOR MISERY

*Bradley has just returned to the apartment he shares with Courtney.*

**Courtney:** You look exhausted, Bradley. Is the elevator out of order again?

**Bradley:** Yes! What an annoyance! I'm totally out of 1. _____. Do you think climbing all those stairs could trigger a heart 2. _____?

**Courtney:** Oh, stop being such a drama queen. We only live on the fourth floor.

**Bradley:** OK. Perhaps that was an 3. _____. But I had never realized what a total pain in the neck it is to take the stairs until today.

**Courtney:** You're just lazy. Laziness can spur creativity though. You know, a French king had the first passenger elevator 4. _____ because his mistress was frustrated with walking up one flight of stairs.

**Bradley:** I wonder how long she had 5. _____ him about the stairs before he had it built.

**Courtney:** Who knows? Her life must have been a lot easier when it was completed, although the servants probably hated it. They had to operate the device by hand.

**Bradley:** What a 6. _____ job!

**Courtney:** No doubt. But luckily, by the 1800s elevators were powered by steam. Then Elisha Otis unveiled an 7. _____ brake system that is still used today.

**Bradley:** He really hit the jackpot with that idea.

**Courtney:** Yeah. Otis's sons carried on his legacy. By 1873, over 2,000 Otis elevators had been 8. _____ across the United States.

**Bradley:** Maybe I should become an elevator engineer. That way, I'll never be tormented by stairs again.

**out of order:** broken

**drama queen:** someone who gets too angry over small problems

**servant:** someone who works and lives in someone else's house

**unveil:** to show

**hit the jackpot:** to make or win a lot of money

**Practice the conversation with your partner.**

## LANGUAGE FOCUS
### Overreacting
### Talking About Annoyances

**Overreacting**

- be/act like a drama queen
- make too much of (*something*)
- blow (*something*) out of proportion
- go overboard

### Task 1
*Rewrite the parts in bold using the expressions. Do not repeat any of your answer choices.*

1. Whenever my daughter doesn't get her way, she **starts kicking and screaming**.
   → Whenever my daughter doesn't get her way, she _____.

2. Most bloggers **exaggerate what they write about**.
   → Most bloggers _____.

3. You should stop **dwelling on your breakup so much**.
   → You should stop _____.

**Talking About Annoyances**

| (*something/someone*) | • be (such) an annoyance<br>• be a (total) pain in the neck<br>• get on (*one's*) nerves |
|---|---|
| (*someone*) | • be/get fed up with (*something/someone*) |

### Task 2
*Fill in the appropriate expressions.*

1. My faulty alarm clock _____ because it always beeps at the wrong time.

2. This stain spray _____! Not only is it difficult to apply, but it also doesn't work well.

3. Todd _____ his battered old car, so he decided to purchase a brand-new one.

### Task 3
*Listen to the audio. Match the speaker with the appropriate statement.*  1-16

Betty

Seth

- I'm growing tired of how unreliable my car is.
- I can't tolerate leaving early to arrive somewhere promptly because I don't have an automobile.
- The primary disadvantage of driving is getting stuck in traffic.
- I get annoyed by drivers who constantly honk their horns.
- In my opinion, public transportation has too many drawbacks.
- Not having a place to sit on a crammed bus makes me feel uncomfortable.

## GRAMMAR | Past Perfect

We can use the past perfect tense to tell a story or to explain how something occurred in sequence. The past perfect is often used with the simple past.

### Usage

| | |
|---|---|
| To express the idea that something happened before another past action or a specific time | • I had to move because my landlord **had increased** my rent.<br>• By 1873, over 2,000 Otis elevators **had been installed** across the United States. |
| To indicate that something began in the past and continued for a period of time | • I **had** never **realized** what a total pain in the neck it is to take the stairs until today.<br>• I wonder how long she **had nagged** him about the stairs before he had it built. |
| To form reported speech after verbs such as *asked, said, thought, told,* and *wondered* | • Candy said that Mike **had relocated** to Hong Kong.<br>• I thought they **had discussed** the terms of the agreement. |

### Simple Past vs. Past Perfect

| Simple Past | Past Perfect |
|---|---|
| We use the simple past to talk about past events in the order they occur. | We look back from one time in the past to tell what has happened previously. |
| • When Miles **looked** out the window, he **noticed** someone stealing his car. He **called** the police immediately. | • Before Christy met Harry, she **had** never **known** what a real partnership was like. |

### Task

*Match the two parts.*

1. I had asked Nancy to write up an estimate of the building costs, _____.
2. Bill was suffering from fatigue _____.
3. Although Sheila had immediately offered to compensate him for the damage, _____ .
4. When they said they owned a cottage, _____.
5. Eunice wasn't able to breathe a sigh of relief _____.
6. Alice had just purchased the house _____.

a. until the doctor informed her that her surgery had been successful
b. I had no idea they were talking about this impressive mansion
c. because he had worked too much overtime
d. but she didn't get the information to me before the meeting
e. when a hurricane destroyed her roof
f. Kent didn't accept until months later

## READING

# Where the Inventors Come From

### BEFORE YOU READ  1-17

*Scan the article below. Write the paragraph number (1-4) next to the matching main idea. There are two extra choices.*

☐ Numerous devices are invented in Japan every year.

☐ Germans have an excellent education system, especially when it comes to science.

☐ Most countries work hard to be considered inventive.

☐ Israel is striving to prove that it can innovate as well as larger countries.

☐ The Japanese are most concerned about the future of robots.

☐ Throughout history, Germans have been responsible for the invention of many useful things.

1   It's hard to imagine that televisions had been unavailable to the public until 100 years ago, but now we can carry portable phones in our pockets. Inventions will continue to change the world, and countries will pull out all the stops to be the most innovative.

### GERMANY

5   Germany had proved its inventiveness long before the modern era. Many inventions that are used every day, including the printing press and the gas-powered engine, can be attributed to German inventors. Also notable
10  are their breakthroughs in the medical and pharmaceutical fields. Have a headache? Aspirin, one of the most commonly used medicines in

the world, was created in this northern European nation. Break a bone? It's because of German ingenuity that we have X-rays.
15 Unsurprisingly, when education systems are ranked, Germany's science programs are frequently placed in the top 10.

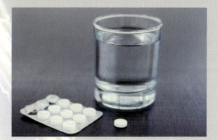

## JAPAN

For years, Japan has been second only to the US in the number of patents filed. Hundreds of thousands of
20 patent applications, from the bizarre to the practical, are submitted each year in this Asian country. Japanese inventors show a talent for the imaginative, but they are perhaps most well-known for their obsession with robots. The
25 robot teacher Saya was an immediate worldwide sensation when "she" was launched. Saya can fluently speak multiple languages and is able to recognize if students make mistakes. One Japanese inventor has even devised a robot with 24 "fingers" that can shampoo, condition, and blow-
30 dry a person's hair.

## ISRAEL

Despite being one of the smallest countries on the planet, Israel is working earnestly to prove that it can be a center for innovation, especially in the
35 technology sector. Israel is already the birthplace of the USB flash drive, a device that has become synonymous with convenient digital storage. Furthermore, network security companies in Israel have gained the reputation of being the best in
40 the industry. In order to spur more development, the Israeli government invests a large percentage

of the nation's GDP in research. Thanks to these funds, Israel boasts one start-up company for every 1,800 people. With all of these independent businesses, this Middle Eastern country is sure to be at the forefront of future technological advancements.

45 Without these countries, we wouldn't have access to many of the conveniences and luxuries that we enjoy today!

# AFTER YOU READ

### A. Vocabulary

*Fill in the blanks with the word choices given. Change the word form if necessary.*

> forefront / attribute / pharmaceutical / breakthrough / submit

1. There have been many _____ in cancer research during the past decade; however, the medical community is still far from finding a cure.

2. Because the number of elderly people is increasing, the _____ industry is creating drugs that tackle their health ailments.

3. The current fad of 3D movies can be _____ to the release of the film *Avatar*.

4. Applications won't be accepted if they're not _____ by the deadline.

5. Japanese automobile companies are at the _____ of the electric car market. Other nations are behind them in terms of development.

### B. Comprehension Check

*Write **G** for Germany, **J** for Japan, or **I** for Israel next to the matching description.*

1. The country is responsible for the invention of what is usually used to treat headaches.

2. The government invests a large amount of money in small enterprises to boost the economy.

3. Scientific achievements are associated with the quality of the education system here.

4. Computer system innovations are some of this country's most notable contributions.

5. The bulk of this nation's inventions take care of tasks that humans would normally complete.

### C. Discussion

*Share your opinion with the class.*

Patent systems have been in use in various countries for hundreds of years. The first patents only granted an inventor exclusivity of rights for a few years, but modern ones can last for decades. Do today's patents give too few or too many rights to their owners? Are there some things that shouldn't be allowed to be patented?

# WRITING

## Unity and Coherence

In a **unified** paragraph, every sentence should be related to the topic.

Look at this topic sentence: The brains of scientists and inventors usually have the most activity occurring on the right side.

Now read the following sentences.

**1** An individual whose right brain is dominant seems to be organized and goal oriented.

**2** The brain is continuously active, never stopping even for a moment.

 **Sentence 1 refers to the topic and sentence 2 does not.**

In a **coherent** paragraph, sentences should logically flow from one idea to the next.

**1** Right-sided thinkers are devoted to solving problems. **2** They are often at risk of collapsing due to an intense workload. **3** Sometimes, they get so focused on resolving other people's issues that they overwork themselves.

 **In this paragraph, sentence 2 should be placed after sentence 3.**

## Task

Write the letter of the sentence next to the main idea it develops.

| | Topic Sentence | Supporting Ideas |
|---|---|---|
| 1. | Helen Keller overcame being blind and deaf to graduate college with honors. | |
| 2. | Sybilla Masters became the first official female inventor in 1715, but women had been inventing before without recognition. | |
| 3. | Gunpei Yokoi created the Game Boy, one of Nintendo's best-selling devices. | |

a. Her patent was unfairly issued in her husband's name, as women weren't allowed to own patents.

b. Since its release in 1980, the game has sold over 118 million units!

c. Anne Sullivan taught her how to speak and read Braille, preparing her for further academic accomplishments.

d. Before this moneymaker, he invented The Ultrahand, the first toy the company ever manufactured.

e. She created a method to preserve corn, a common dish for American people.

f. By age seven, she had invented over 60 signs that enabled her to communicate with others.

# EXTRA WRITING PRACTICE

## BEFORE YOU WRITE

Visit the site http://en.wikipedia.org/wiki/Velcro to research the topics below. Write four related sentences about the uses of Velcro.

| | |
|---|---|
| **The Creation of Velcro** | 1. George de Mestral, a Swiss electrical engineer, was inspired to invent Velcro in 1948 after picking off seeds that were hooked into his pants.<br>2. He had noticed that the seeds were strongly attached to the loops of the fabric.<br>3. At first, he copied this design idea using cotton, but it weakened quickly, so he began using synthetic fibers instead.<br>4. Because of this and other delays, it took 10 years to create a process that worked. He received a patent for his invention in 1955. |
| **The Uses of Velcro** | 1.<br>2.<br>3.<br>4. |

## WRITE IT UP

Complete the passage. Then write another 140-word essay about the uses of Velcro. Make sure the flow of your piece is coherent.

### Taking a Cue from Mother Nature

George de Mestral, a Swiss electrical engineer, invented Velcro in 1948. He was inspired after _____
_____.

He realized this idea could be an effective method of fastening clothes. At first, he copied the design using cotton, _____
_____. Then he had to create a special loom to weave the Velcro. _____
_____.

Now, people all over the world use Velcro!

### Velcro Is Amazing!

_____
_____
_____
_____
_____

# UNIT 5

# The World of Food

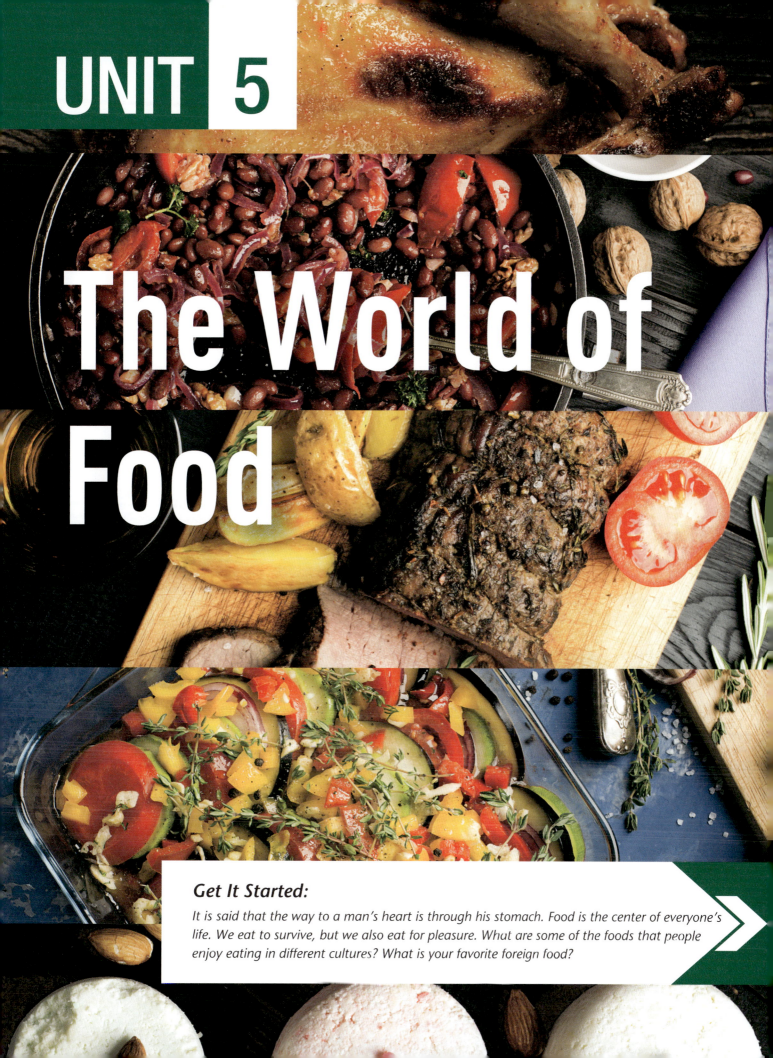

**Get It Started:**
It is said that the way to a man's heart is through his stomach. Food is the center of everyone's life. We eat to survive, but we also eat for pleasure. What are some of the foods that people enjoy eating in different cultures? What is your favorite foreign food?

# VOCABULARY

## Task 1

*Match the following words with their correct definitions.*  CD 1-18

1. adjust      _____
2. greasy      _____
3. eligible    _____
4. irritate    _____
5. crucial     _____
6. nutritious  _____
7. starving    _____

a. to make a part of your body hurt
b. very hungry
c. to change something slightly to make it work better
d. oily
e. (of food) containing many of the substances which help the body to grow
f. allowed to do something
g. important

## Task 2

*Fill in the blanks with these words in the box.*

> simmer / heat / season / bake / boil / stir

### Mama Celia's Lasagna

**Step I:** In a pan, quickly brown the Italian sausage with the onion and garlic. 1. _____ in crushed tomatoes.

2. _____ with salt, pepper, and Italian seasoning.

3. _____ for 1 1/2 hours.

**Step II:** 4. _____ the noodles for 10 minutes. Drain them and rinse with cold water. In a bowl, combine cheese with egg, parsley, and salt.

**Step III:** 5. _____ the oven to 375 degrees F. Layer the meat and tomato sauce, noodles, and cheese and egg mixture in a baking dish. Repeat until all the ingredients are used.

**Step IV:** 6. _____ in the oven for 30 minutes. Allow to cool slightly before serving.

# LISTENING & SPEAKING

## A. Comprehension Check

*Listen to the conversation and check **T** if the statement is true, **F** if it's false.*  CD 1-19

1. T ☐ F ☐ Claire is so hungry that she could eat a huge amount of food.
2. T ☐ F ☐ Jeff is under so much stress that he cannot stop eating snacks.
3. T ☐ F ☐ Claire can hardly concentrate on her study without eating something.
4. T ☐ F ☐ Jeff hasn't submitted his thesis yet, so he has to finish it as soon as possible.
5. T ☐ F ☐ Cindy suggests that Claire stop eating oily and sweet food.

50

B. **Partial Dictation**

Listen again and fill in the blanks.  1-19

# Stress Eating

Claire sits down with Cindy and Jeff at their school cafeteria.

**Cindy:** Wow. That's an enormous plate of food.

**Claire:** I'm 1. _____. Lately, I feel like I could eat a horse!

**Jeff:** Really? I've been eating like a bird. My stomach seems to be tied up in knots.

**Cindy:** You two sound like you're suffering from stress. Claire, when your body is under pressure, it needs 2. _____ energy to perform, so you wolf down food constantly.

**Claire:** If I don't nibble on something while I'm studying, I can 3. _____ concentrate. Maybe if I weren't so busy, I wouldn't gorge myself.

**Jeff:** What about me? Normally, I have a soft spot for sweets. Now I just don't want to eat them at all. I feel as full as a tick.

**Claire:** Do you have any 4. _____ assignment approaching?

**Jeff:** I just 5. _____ my thesis. If I hadn't completed it before the deadline, I wouldn't have been eligible to graduate. Even though it's finished, I'm nervous about the results.

**Cindy:** Anxiety can 6. _____ your stomach. That's why you feel uncomfortably full even if you haven't eaten anything.

**Jeff:** Yuck. How can we eliminate these issues?

**Cindy:** 7. _____ your eating habits can lessen stress. You have to go cold turkey on that greasy and sugary food.

**Claire:** But I can't resist chips and pastries.

**Cindy:** Calm down. 8. _____ food can be tasty, too. Plus, many chip manufacturers make baked chips. They're not a healthy food, but they're better than the alternative.

**Claire:** What a relief!

**Practice the conversation with your partner.**

*eat a horse:* to eat a lot

*wolf down:* to eat something very quickly

*nibble:* to eat something by taking very small bites

*gorge:* to eat something very quickly

*go cold turkey on:* to stop completely

# LANGUAGE FOCUS
Talking About Your Appetite
Expressing Anxiety

**Talking About Your Appetite**

| Feeling Hungry | Feeling Full |
|---|---|
| • be starving/starved | • be as full as a tick |
| • could eat a horse | • couldn't eat another bite |
| • (*one's*) stomach feel like a bottomless pit | • be stuffed to the gills |

## Task 1

*Pair up with a classmate and use the expressions above to discuss the following situations.*

1. Right after a hearty lunch
2. After gobbling up a large pizza
3. Following a hard workout
4. After enjoying Thanksgiving dinner

*Example*

• Right before lunchtime, I'**m starving**, but after eating a hearty lunch, I **feel stuffed to the gills**.

## Task 2

*Listen to the audio. Check **T** if the statement is true, **F** if it's false.*   1-20

1. T ☐  F ☐  Doug has a hard time with Egyptian politics.
2. T ☐  F ☐  Doug isn't concerned about delivering a marketing presentation.
3. T ☐  F ☐  Emma finds her math exam less stressful than the business speech.
4. T ☐  F ☐  Emma doesn't feel relief after taking her math final exam.

**Expressing Anxiety**

| Feeling Anxious | • (*one's*) stomach be (tied up) in knots<br>• have a knot in (*one's*) stomach<br>• have/get butterflies in (*one's*) stomach |
|---|---|
| Waiting to Find out Something Important | • be (sitting) on pins and needles |
| Expecting Something Bad to Happen | • be/feel on edge |

## Task 3

*Fill in the appropriate expressions. Some blanks may have more than one possible answer.*

1. My son Jimmy should receive notification about his acceptance into Harvard today. We're both _____!
2. Ever since I saw that scary movie about a plane crash, I've _____ _____ about flying.
3. I can't eat anything. I'm so nervous about this test that my _____ _____.

52

# GRAMMAR | Conditionals

The first conditional and second conditional are used to speak about the present or the future. The third conditional is used to express opinions about things in the past.

## Summary

| | First Conditional | Second Conditional | Third Conditional |
|---|---|---|---|
| **Nature** | possible condition | unreal situation | unreal situation |
| **Time** | present or future | present | past |
| **Form** | If + simple present, S + will/can/might + V | If + simple past, S +would/should/might/could + V | If + past perfect, S + would/should/might/could have + past participle. |
| **Example** | • If I **don't nibble** on something while I'm studying, I **can** barely **concentrate**. | • If I **weren't** so busy, I **wouldn't gorge** myself. | • If I **hadn't completed** it before the deadline, I **wouldn't have been** eligible to graduate. |

## Mixed Tense

When the time of the *if* clause is different from the one of the *main clause*, it's possible to have several types of mixed conditional sentences.

| If Clause | Main Clause |
|---|---|
| present | past |
| If she **spoke** Russian, | she **would have had** an easier time in Moscow. |
| past | present |
| If I **had seen** a doctor, | my head **wouldn't hurt** so much now. |
| past | future |
| If I **had known** you planned to visit Grandpa tomorrow, | I **would be going** with you. |

## Task

*Use the correct form of the verbs in parentheses to complete the sentences.*

1. If everyone took public transportation, there _____ (**be**) a lot less air pollution.

2. If you _____ (**not wear**) those rugged clothes to the interview, you might have secured the job.

3. I _____ (**not open**) the document if you had notified me that it was regarding a personal matter.

4. If you _____ (**exercise**) regularly, it might help to boost your immune system and enhance overall fitness.

5. Cindy spent significant time commuting by bus this morning. She would have driven her car if it _____ (**not break**) down.

6. If only I had known how important Mr. Lennon was to the community, I _____ (**dedicate**) today's speech to him.

53

# READING

### BEFORE YOU READ  1-21

*If action is not taken, the world might face a global food crisis. Check the most practical solutions to this problem.*

- ☐ Reduce meat consumption
- ☐ Increase your water intake
- ☐ Grow your own fruit and vegetables
- ☐ Eat two portions of oily fish a week
- ☐ Cultivate produce indoors
- ☐ Adopt a wholly vegetarian diet
- ☐ Make meat without animals
- ☐ Stock up on canned food

*Keep reading to find out more.*

# The Future of Food

1   Experts predict that nine billion people will populate the Earth by 2050. Medical advancements have caused the average life span and birth survival rate to surge. These are outstanding successes, but they've created a problem: as farmland disappears due to overpopulation, what will people
5   eat? If scientists don't discover an answer, the world might face a food crisis. Thankfully, there are possible solutions.

Vertical farming is the concept of cultivating food within skyscrapers. Using advanced greenhouse
10   technology, it's feasible to produce fruit and vegetables indoors. If this idea becomes reality, it will require significantly less land than fields. In fact, a 30-story building with a five-acre-wide base could yield a yearly harvest equivalent to 2,400 acres. This exceeds
15   traditional farming output because plants inside a building are sheltered from the weather. With climate, water, and light control, the effects of temperature,

droughts, and cloudy days are eliminated. Crops can be grown year-round. It's also beneficial that vertical farms can be constructed in close proximity to urban areas. As much as 30 percent of crops are wasted due to spoilage during transport. With a shorter distance between food and consumers, harvested produce can be delivered while it's still fresh.

Indoor plant production has already been successfully implemented in Japan. The country has about 50 fully operational factories that grow everything from lettuce to strawberries. These facilities pump out food two to four times faster than traditional farming. When functioning at full capacity, they can produce up to three million vegetables per year!

Meat, on the other hand, will be trickier to copy, yet it is as essential as plants. Livestock consume more energy per food unit than any plant crop. For example, one pound of beef requires 16 pounds of grain and 2,500 gallons of water. Obviously, if everyone became a vegetarian, this would no longer be a problem. But a campaign to convince billions of omnivorous* humans to stop eating meat wouldn't stand a chance. Thus, scientists are experimenting to create meat. To accomplish this, cells are taken from live animals and stored to grow into meat over time. In theory, this process could meet global demands. However, the idea is still in its infancy.

Until scientists achieve artificial food production, you should consider restricting your meat consumption and growing produce in your own yard. The world of 2050 will thank you!

[Note] *omnivorous: eating meat as well as vegetables

# AFTER YOU READ

## A. Vocabulary

*Fill in the blanks with the word choices given. Change the word form if necessary.*

> **span / yield / infancy / exceed / surge**

1. The number of applicants for the medical program _____ last year after the school was ranked first in the nation.

2. If you double the amount of the ingredients, the recipe will _____ twice as many cookies.

3. You should not _____ the highway's speed limit; otherwise, you might get fined.

4. Due to the advent of computer technology, the younger generation tends to have a short attention _____.

5. Although the cancer-screening device is in its _____, researchers hope that it will be an effective detection method.

## B. Comprehension Check

*Circle the answers.*

1. What is said about the world's population?
   a. It will soar because medical knowledge has expanded.
   b. It will stay constant because of a lack of resources available.
   c. It will increase since the birth rate is surging everywhere.
   d. It will decrease due to insufficient land.

2. Which statement is true?
   a. Farming must take place outdoors.
   b. Growing crops indoors is advantageous for producing food.
   c. Vertical farming won't eliminate the need for regular farmland.
   d. Weather conditions will need to be duplicated inside produce factories.

3. Why does some produce never get sold to consumers?
   a. Many tests must be done to see how production can be improved.
   b. 30 percent of the crops are picked before they are fully mature.
   c. Produce grown in vertical farms hasn't yet been approved for consumption.
   d. A large amount of the crops go bad before they arrive at stores.

4. What can we infer from the article?
   a. Meat is more readily available than vegetables.
   b. Humans despise the idea of growing their own produce.
   c. Most people enjoy eating both meat and vegetables.
   d. Growing fruit indoors is much slower than normal methods.

## C. Discussion

*Share your opinion with the class.*

> In the past decade, the cost of oil has increased by approximately $100 per barrel. This has caused food prices to rise dramatically. The World Food Bank estimates that the higher cost of food has pushed 44 million more people into poverty. Which practice(s) mentioned in the article could eliminate this problem?

# WRITING

### Generalizations and Examples

The main idea of an essay or a paragraph is often a **generalization**. As the passage progresses, the writer supports the general statement with increasingly **specific examples**.

Desserts are fattening. (general)
→ Because recipes call for butter and sugar, sweets contain many calories. (specific)
→ One slice of apple pie with ice cream can have as many as 550 calories! (more specific)

### Task 1
*Cross out the sentence in the paragraph below that is not specific enough.*

My friend Ross gets a thrill out of eating spicy food. When a dish makes his eyes burn and his nose run, he relishes it! That's why Indian food is his favorite type of exotic cuisine. For example, he likes many Indian dishes.

### Task 2
*Read the general statement below and write two supporting examples. Example 2 should be more specific.*

| Many foods have a hearty amount of protein. | → 1. _____<br>→ 2. _____ |
|---|---|
| Critics believe that Hollywood is losing its originality. | → 1. _____<br>→ 2. _____ |
| Different countries have varying opinions about when their citizens can be considered adults. | → 1. _____<br>→ 2. _____ |

# EXTRA WRITING PRACTICE

## BEFORE YOU WRITE
*Read the topic sentence below and think of two more specific examples.*

 **Main Idea** — While most people don't consider mealtime a competitive event, eating competitions take place around the world.

→ **Support** — Nathan's Hot Dog Eating Contest has been held every year since 1970. Competitors have to consume as many hot dogs as they can in 10 minutes. ESPN televises the event live!

→ **Support**

→ **Support**

## WRITE IT UP
Write a 140-word argumentative essay for or against eating competitions. Include the conditional structures you've learned.

**Title:** _____ (Be creative.)

While most people don't consider mealtime a competitive event, eating competitions take place around the world.

**Introduction:** Introduce your argument.

**Body:** Begin each paragraph with a generalization and then include specific examples.

**Conclusion:** Restate your position.

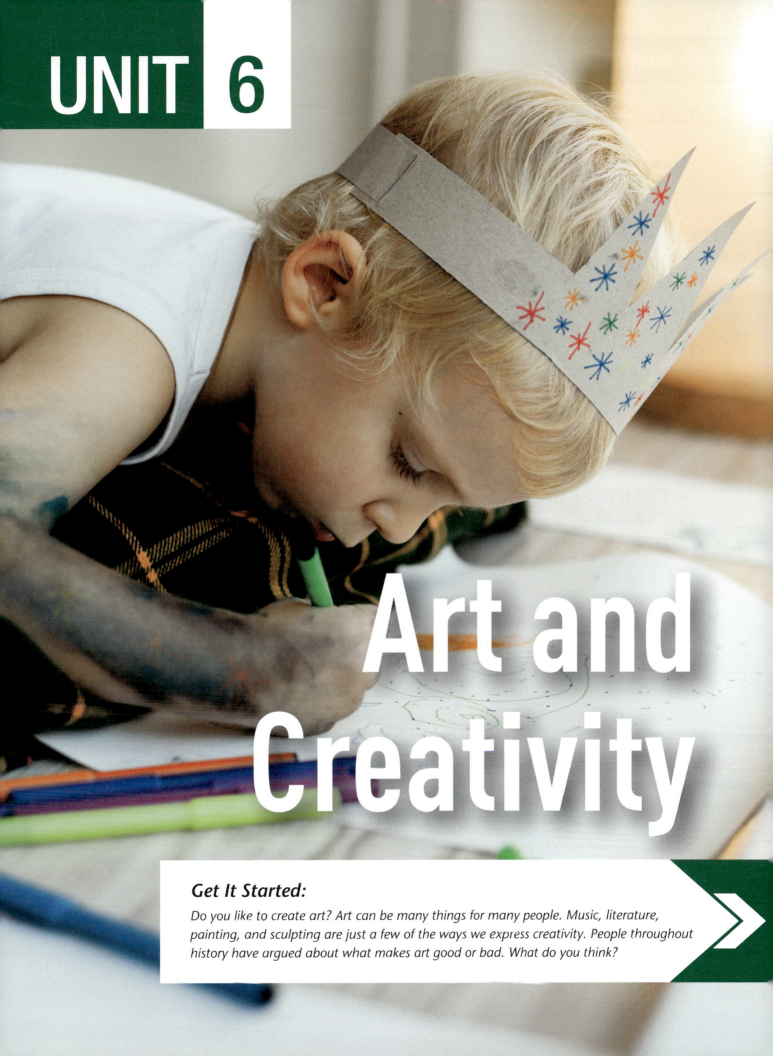

# UNIT 6

# Art and Creativity

*Get It Started:*
Do you like to create art? Art can be many things for many people. Music, literature, painting, and sculpting are just a few of the ways we express creativity. People throughout history have argued about what makes art good or bad. What do you think?

# VOCABULARY

## Task 1

*Match the following words with their correct definitions.* 🎧 1-22

1. temporary _____
2. experimental _____
3. comprise _____
4. novelty _____
5. smashing _____
6. affordable _____
7. contemporary _____

a. not expensive
b. using new ideas or methods
c. extremely good
d. modern
e. the quality of being new, unusual, and interesting
f. lasting only for a short time
g. to have as parts or members

## Task 2

*Fill in the blanks with the correct forms of the words provided.*

subjective / acclaimed / complement / exhibit / accessible / sculpture

Metropolitan Transportation Authority (MTA)
Arts for Transit

### CALL FOR IMAGES

The Metropolitan Transportation Authority seeks to commission new artwork for various stations. Because of the ❶ _____ nature of art, submissions will be reviewed by a panel that is composed of collectors, gallery managers, and other art professionals.

**Guidelines**
- Please keep in mind that your work will be fully ❷ _____ to your fellow citizens. As such, work should represent the spirit of New York and ❸ _____ our city's international image.
- All work must be original and share no similarity with any other productions.
- Acceptable mediums are as follows: ❹ _____, photographs, and pottery.

Having your work displayed in the MTA is a significant step in ❺ _____ your art, as many of the pieces have become critically ❻ _____. Submit today!

Photo: Flickr / nycstreets

# LISTENING & SPEAKING

## A. Comprehension Check

*Listen to the conversation and check **T** if the statement is true, **F** if it's false.* 🎧 1-23

1. T ☐ F ☐ Amy and Alyssa aren't concerned about their vacation expenditures.
2. T ☐ F ☐ The Sarasota Chalk Festival features artwork that will wash away easily.
3. T ☐ F ☐ The world's biggest arts festival is located in the Northwestern United States.
4. T ☐ F ☐ If the girls would like to see the works of Shakespeare, they would have to travel to Scotland.
5. T ☐ F ☐ They couldn't reach an agreement on which festival to attend.

## B. Partial Dictation

Listen again and fill in the blanks.  1-23

# ARTS FESTIVALS

*Amy and Alyssa are chatting in their dorm room.*

**Amy:** I'm ecstatic that we can finally make plans for our fall break!

**Alyssa:** Me, too. There are multiple arts festivals going on, and I know some that 1. _____ break the bank.

**Amy:** Great! I've been thinking about which ones to attend. Fill me in.

**Alyssa:** There's the Sarasota Chalk Festival in Florida. I went there with my parents last year. It was a 2. _____ success. It will certainly knock your socks off.

**Amy:** Cool. Tell me more about it.

**Alyssa:** Artists draw designs on sidewalks with 3. _____ materials like chalk.

**Amy:** Doesn't that wear off?

**Alyssa:** Sure, but that's the 4. _____ of it. It's thrilling to experience what the artists are able to do in the moment.

**Amy:** Watching people draw on the ground sounds as exciting as watching grass grow.

**Alyssa:** What about the Fringe? It's the world's largest arts festival and is 5. _____ of performing arts.

**Amy:** Sounds intriguing. What types of acts are included?

**Alyssa:** Usually theater, but dance and music are also featured. Ticketed events range from Shakespearean classics to spectacular 6. _____ works, and even experimental plays. Shoot! I just remembered it's held in Scotland. I wonder if the flights are 7. _____.

**Amy:** Nope. They would cost a pretty penny.

**Alyssa:** Let's try Bumbershoot in Seattle then. This gigantic arts event 8. _____ circus acts, ongoing street theater, independent short films, and poetry readings.

**Amy:** Wow. Sounds like a winner!

**ecstatic:** extremely happy

**break the bank:** to cost a lot of money

**fill someone in:** to tell someone about recent events

**knock one's socks off:** to surprise someone very much

**intriguing:** very interesting

**a pretty penny:** a lot of money

*Practice the conversation with your partner.*

# LANGUAGE FOCUS | Discussing Prices / Describing Amazing and Boring Things

## Discussing Prices

| Affordable | Expensive |
|---|---|
| • won't break the bank<br>• cost next to nothing<br>• be easy on (*one's*) pocket | • cost (*someone*) a pretty penny<br>• be highway robbery<br>• pay through the nose |

### Task 1
*Fill in the blanks with the expressions above. There may be more than one possible answer.*

1. **A:** You don't want to shop here. You will have to _____ for the clothes in this store.
   **B:** You're right. Let's go somewhere with merchandise that _____.

2. **A:** Check out Luke's new car! That's a brand-new model. It must have _____.
   **B:** Nope. He struck a bargain, so he got it at a good price.

### Task 2
*Correct the list based on the audio.*  1-24

| Ryan & Lauren's Christmas List |||
|---|---|---|
| **Parents** | **Other Family Members** | **Friends** |
| • TV show box set<br>• potted mint<br>• *The New York Times* subscription<br>• _____ | • ~~Gucci handbag~~<br>• _____ | • scarves<br>• basketball tickets<br>• _____ |

## Describing Amazing and Boring Things

| Amazing | Boring |
|---|---|
| • knock (*one's*) socks off<br>• take (*one's*) breath away<br>• give *someone* goose bumps | • be as exciting as watching grass grow<br>• be like watching paint dry<br>• bore *someone* to tears |

### Task 3
*Fill in the blanks below. Use different expressions for each blank.*

1. Phil hiked Mt. Fuji last weekend. The majestic view from atop the mountain _____.
2. Clint always tells lame jokes, and listening to them is _____.
3. The Great Pyramid of Giza in Egypt was built more than 4,500 years ago and remains largely intact. Seeing it _____!

# GRAMMAR | Noun Clauses

Unit 6

A noun clause is connected to an independent clause and serves the same purpose in a sentence as a noun.

## Form

| Signal Word | Example |
|---|---|
| that | • The teacher explained **(that) Korea is a peninsula**. |
| if/whether | • I wonder **if the flights are affordable**. |
| wh- word + to V | • My coworker asked me **how to use the copy machine**. |
| wh- or wh-ever word + S + V | • It's thrilling to experience **what the artists are able to do in the moment**. |

## Sentence Pattern

Some verbs and adjectives are often followed by noun clauses. In this structure, the verb in the noun clause usually stays in its base form.

| S | advise, ask, demand, insist, propose, order, urge, recommend, request, suggest . . . | (that) + noun clause |
|---|---|---|
| It is | crucial, essential, imperative, important, critical, necessary, vital . . . | (that) + noun clause |

ex. It is essential that you use celery in this traditional Chinese dish.

## Task 1

*Put the letter of the appropriate noun clause in the sentence.*

| Sentence |
|---|
| 1. As the singer hasn't signed a contract, _____ is still being discussed. |
| 2. He advises _____ because they are fragile. |
| 3. This piece of jade is precious. The company will sell it to _____. |
| 4. Scientists aren't completely certain _____. |
| 5. The principal is waiting to see _____. |

| Noun Clause |
|---|
| a. whoever offers the highest price |
| b. when she will release her latest CD |
| c. that these items be handled with extra care |
| d. if Debbie can justify skipping all her classes yesterday |
| e. how many black holes move through our galaxy |

## Task 2

*Fix the errors in the sentences.*

1. The company demands if the man stopping making these false allegations.

   _____

2. Where building the new nuclear power plant will be decided via a public poll.

   _____

3. Carlo doesn't know why does his father get so passionate when they discuss religion.

   _____

63

# READING

## BEFORE YOU READ  1-25

*What do you think **artist-in-residence programs** are? Scan the article and choose the appropriate description.*

a. Artist-in-residence programs increase arts education in schools through free workshops.

b. Each program is designed to provide facilities, such as studios or rehearsal spaces, for visiting artists to focus on their art.

c. In most cases, artists are paid to come and help cities or towns that need visual or cultural improvement.

# Where Have All the Artists Gone?

1   When government budgets need to be cut, arts programs are usually the first expenses to go. However, in some places, extra money is being allocated to increase artistic projects rather than cancel them.

## Laois County Council Residency

5   The Arts Council of Ireland created the Arthouse Studios in Laois County in 2011 to encourage local artists to sharpen their skills. The Arthouse Studios include four personal studios, two with accommodation, as well as an exhibition space and a rehearsal area. Painters, filmmakers, and sculptors are all eligible candidates for the available spots. After approval, artists can make use of the studios for free for three months to a year; however, it is required that they give complimentary
10  workshops to members of the community.

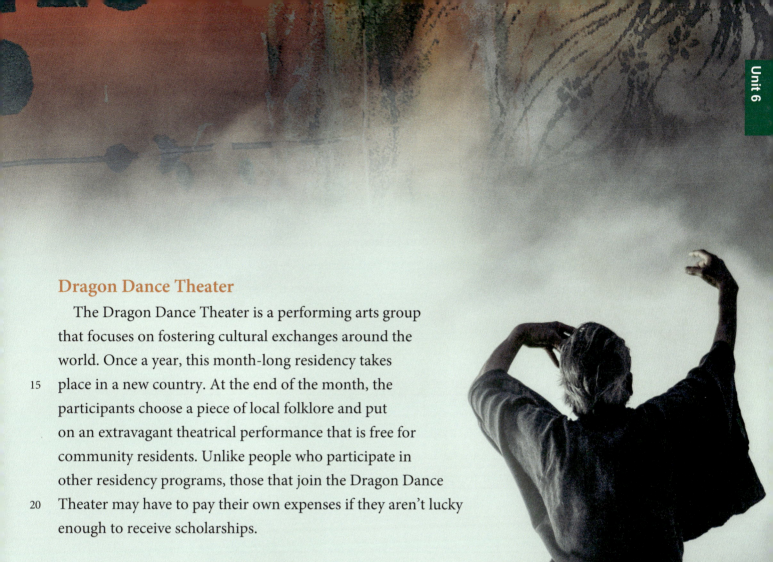

### Dragon Dance Theater

The Dragon Dance Theater is a performing arts group that focuses on fostering cultural exchanges around the world. Once a year, this month-long residency takes place in a new country. At the end of the month, the participants choose a piece of local folklore and put on an extravagant theatrical performance that is free for community residents. Unlike people who participate in other residency programs, those that join the Dragon Dance Theater may have to pay their own expenses if they aren't lucky enough to receive scholarships.

### Instinc Air

The artist-in-residence program, INSTINC AIR, was established in Singapore by a local artist to open networking opportunities for him and his peers. INSTINC AIR offers visiting artists one-month or three-month residencies. Applicants' evaluations for admittance are based on the quality of their previous work and their commitment to further arts programs in their homelands. The 12 artists that are accepted each year have their living costs covered and also get their artwork publicized!

More and more city governments have come to realize that the arts are too important to eliminate; rather, they should be cultivated. Because of this, the chances for professional artists to energize their communities are constantly growing. If you are a fan of art, why not check for an artist-in-residence program in your area? You may be able to attend free classes or seminars.

# AFTER YOU READ

## A. Vocabulary

*Fill in the blanks with the word choices given. Change the word form if necessary.*

> admittance / complimentary / eligible / folklore / foster

1. Each guest in the presidential suite is given a _____ breakfast.

2. A weekend trip was planned in order to _____ morale in the office.

3. Native American _____ can be heard during the festival.

4. My _____ into the program isn't guaranteed.

5. In most nations, citizens are _____ to vote when they turn 18.

## B. Comprehension Check

*Answer the questions.*

1. Who founded the Arthouse Studios?

2. What is the main feature of the performances staged by the Dragon Dance Theater?

3. Why is admittance into the INSTINC AIR program competitive?

4. What is the author's opinion of artist-in-residence programs?

## C. Discussion

*Share your opinion with the class.*

The Village of the Arts is a large art colony in Florida, USA. There are over 200 homes with attached art studios in the area, and the residents receive aid from nearby cities. In return, the artists hold free exhibitions. Do you think it's worthwhile for governments to promote such places? What benefits do they have for the community?

# WRITING

## The Process Analysis Essay

In a process analysis essay, a writer instructs the reader how to do something.

**Guidelines**

☑ **Explain the procedure.** Describe each necessary step.

☑ **Use chronological order.** List directions in the sequence they should be completed.

| Time Words |
|---|
| then, last, once, eventually, beforehand, afterwards, finally, during, when, as, first, second, after that, later |

☑ **Mention any needed supplies.** Note if anything should be purchased beforehand.

☑ **Warn the reader of any difficulties.** Offer a solution.

☑ **If possible, give examples.** Personal stories will make the process more interesting.

## Task

Arrange the following sentences in chronological order. Use the time words as clues.

| | |
|---|---|
| _1_ | Do you enjoy drawing landscapes but have trouble creating realistic trees? |
| ___ | Then follow these simple steps! |
| ___ | I start with two vertical lines for the trunk and three circles of varied size on top for the vegetation. |
| _4_ | **Once** you have these, sketch the tree's basic outline. |
| ___ | **Secondly**, begin to draw branches. |
| ___ | **After that**, draw in the leaves. |
| _7_ | But, unless it's winter, this won't look like a genuine tree without leaves! |
| ___ | Purchase two pencils—one with a thin point and another with a thick tip **beforehand**. |
| _9_ | **Afterwards**, erase some of the branches so that there are only a few spots of branches showing through. |
| ___ | And voila—your masterpiece is complete! |
| _11_ | Remember that it's impossible to recreate every individual leaf! |
| ___ | So **next**, sketch the border of the leaves. |
| ___ | Instead, aim for leaving an impression. |
| _14_ | Determine which side of the tree is turned away from the sun, and then shade it with the thick-pointed pencil. |
| ___ | **Finally**, turn on the sunlight with shadows. |
| _16_ | Display the drawing to show off your talent to all your friends. |

# EXTRA WRITING PRACTICE

## BEFORE YOU WRITE

*If you organized an art club on campus, what would you need to do? Finish each step below and come up with a few original ideas.*

### ORGANIZING AN ART CLUB

**1** Get the school's administration to recognize your club. This will make you eligible for funding and give you the privilege of utilizing school facilities to host meetings.

**2** Publicize the club by hanging flyers, posting on the school's online forum, and making announcements before your classes.

**3** Recruit people who _____.

**4** Elect leaders to _____.

**5** Create a statement of purpose so _____.

## WRITE IT UP

Use your ideas from above to write a 140-word process analysis essay. Remember to transition with time words and use noun clauses whenever possible.

### Title: Organizing an Art Club

**Introduction:** Get readers' attention.
→ Obsessed by art but not an acclaimed artist? Launch an art club at your school. It's not as complicated as it sounds—you might even have a blast!

**Body:** Give directions and warn of any problems. →

**Conclusion:** Use a clincher. →

# UNIT 7

# Going for Gold

**Get It Started:**

*Sports have evolved over the years. In ancient times, only men were allowed to play; now, even people with disabilities can become Olympic champions. Sports challenge the body and the mind and are important in all societies. How do you put your body to the test?*

# VOCABULARY

## Task 1
Match the following words with their correct definitions.

1. gene _____
2. qualify _____
3. preliminary _____
4. extraordinary _____
5. rigorous _____
6. endurance _____
7. boost _____

a. coming before a more important action or event
b. very severe
c. to improve or increase something
d. very special
e. to succeed in getting into a competition
f. a part of the DNA in a cell that controls physical development, behavior, etc.
g. the ability to continue doing something difficult over a long period of time

## Task 2
Complete the sentences with the correct forms of the words provided.

> stability / forbid / accomplished / stretch / able-bodied

1. Females were excluded from the ancient Olympic Games. They were _____ from watching or participating in the events.
2. A member of Hollywood's elite, Meryl Streep, is one of the most _____ actresses.
3. Pregnant women wear pants with flexible elastic waists. This allows the pants to _____.
4. Shoes with wider heels provide greater _____ for the wearer, which is essential for maintaining balance while walking.
5. All the _____ people prepared the city for the flood. The volunteers had to be fit because they were required to lift heavy objects.

# LISTENING & SPEAKING

## A. Comprehension Check
Listen to the conversation and circle the answers.

1. Why does Stephen feel nervous?
   a. He was not born to be an elite athlete.
   b. Other competitors could outperform him.
   c. His coach keeps discouraging him.

2. What sports equipment will Stephen use?
   a. He will want a bicycle and a helmet.
   b. He and his teammates will need oars.
   c. He must wear a swimsuit and goggles.

3. According to the conversation, why are some athletes more successful than others?
   a. Outstanding athletes have genes that improve how their bodies function.
   b. Researchers have studied their genes to formulate better training programs.
   c. After preliminary competitions, athletes plan an interval of rest.

4. What does ATP do that is beneficial to an athlete?
   a. ATP is important for pumping oxygen through the body quickly.
   b. Having high levels of ATP will allow the muscles to function efficiently.
   c. A person with a high amount of ATP will need to work harder.

B. **Partial Dictation**

Listen again and fill in the blanks.  1-27

# Athletic Genetics

Stephen and his coach are in the locker room before a big competition.

**Stephen:** Coach, I feel like I have butterflies in my stomach.

**Coach:** Calm down, kid. You've got this in the bag.

**Stephen:** I don't know.

**Coach:** Remember when you 1. _____ for this race? Your scores were off the charts! You made the cut, no problem.

**Stephen:** Sure, I may have been the star of the 2. _____ competitions and semifinals, but these are the state finals. Some of those other contestants could totally overtake me and win. They look superhuman.

**Coach:** Relax. You've been endowed with some extraordinary 3. _____.

**Stephen:** Like what?

**Coach:** Researchers have discovered that elite athletes who are born with special genes usually exceed performance 4. _____.

**Stephen:** What do you mean by *special genes*?

**Coach:** OK, let me explain. Champion cyclists and rowers have genes that provide maximum aerobic capacity. These genes can boost their 5. _____ levels. Athletes' bodies are also better able to create ATP, which enhances muscular movement. It's 6. _____ to marathon runners.

**Stephen:** So what? I'm a swimmer!

**Coach:** Remarkable athletes start with impressive genes. Plus, you've had 7. _____ training. You're not going to fall flat on your face. But what's even more significant is mental strength.

**Stephen:** Mental strength?

**Coach:** The mind controls the body and helps it deliver an optimum performance. So restrain your 8. _____ and get excited.

**Stephen:** All right. Let's do this!

**have butterflies in one's stomach:** to feel nervous

**off the charts:** extremely high in level

**make the cut:** to reach the required standard

**be endowed with:** to naturally have a particular feature, quality, etc.

**ATP:** = Adenosine triphosphate (the source of energy that keeps everything going)

**fall flat on one's face:** to not have the result you want or expect

*Practice the conversation with your partner.*

## LANGUAGE FOCUS | Talking About Natural Talents
## Qualifying

### Talking About Natural Talents

| (someone) | be endowed with<br>be born with<br>be blessed with | (talent) |
|-----------|---------------------------------|----------|
| (someone) | be a born/gifted/natural | (noun) |
| (talent) | come naturally to | (someone) |

### Task 1

*With a partner, create short dialogs with the expressions above and the words provided.*

| | |
|---|---|
| equations | public speaking |
| musical aptitude | salesperson |
| languages | green thumb |
| leader | theatrical talent |

**Example**

A: Jeff is good at solving equations.
   He must have **been born with** those skills.
B: I know. Math just seems to **come naturally to** him.

### Qualifying

- make the cut
- measure up
- fit the bill
- cut the mustard
- make the grade

### Task 2

*Revise the parts in bold based on the audio. Decide if the candidates are qualified or not.* 🎧 1-28

| Candidate | Comments | Qualified? | |
|-----------|----------|-----------|---|
| Charlotte | Her ~~courtesy~~ will be a beneficial asset to our team.<br>*experience* | ☑ Qualified | ☐ Disqualified |
| Pete | They learned he had been **promoted at his other job.** | ☐ Qualified | ☐ Disqualified |
| Bob | He **acted calmly** until he cursed loudly during the interview. | ☐ Qualified | ☐ Disqualified |
| Aaron | He presented himself well and was wearing **a pair of sloppy jeans and a T-shirt.** | ☐ Qualified | ☐ Disqualified |
| Suzie | She is inexperienced but will probably improve **over time.** | ☐ Qualified | ☐ Disqualified |

# GRAMMAR | Adjective Clauses

Unit 7

Adjective clauses have a subject and verb. They start with a relative pronoun and are used as adjectives to modify nouns.

## Relative Pronouns

| Pronoun | Use | Example |
|---------|-----|---------|
| who | subject pronoun for people | Gerhard, **who** is one of our campaigners, lives in Munich. |
| whom | object pronoun for people | Ellie, with **whom** Roy is on good terms, opposes this proposal. |
| whose | possession for people and things | Are you the person **whose** baggage was stolen yesterday? |
| which | subject or object pronoun for things | Nikita has a parrot **which** is able to say some words in Russian. |
| that | subject or object pronoun for people and things | Champion cyclists and rowers have genes **that** provide maximum aerobic capacity. |

**Usage**   **That** is more appropriate than **which** after certain pronouns and superlative nouns.
- *Everything* **that** I had on my hard drive was lost when my computer got a virus.
- That is probably the *worst* catastrophe **that** I have ever witnessed!

## Types of Adjective Clauses

| Type | Usage | Examples |
|------|-------|----------|
| nonrestrictive clauses (use **who** or **which**) | These clauses provide **extra information** about the noun but are not necessary. They are normally set off by commas. | • Annabel, **who** is sitting at the end of the table, is a vegetarian. She won't eat this tuna.<br>• Athletes' bodies are better able to create ATP, **which** enhances muscular movement. |
| restrictive clauses (use **who**, **which** or **that**) | These clauses provide **necessary information** about the noun. They are not set off by commas. | • Mr. Friess is a friend **who** seldom complains about anything.<br>• Homes **that** were damaged by the natural disaster will be repaired for free. |

## Task

*Combine the two sentences by using the second sentence as an adjective clause.*

1. Claude is making a large profit on the stock market. Claude studied economics in college.

   _____

2. People should sign up for this course. These people should want to get some vigorous exercise.

   _____

3. Sam saved two seats so he could sit with his classmate. He met that classmate during orientation.

   _____

4. The musician's debut took place at the national theater. His debut received positive feedback.

   _____

# READING

### BEFORE YOU READ    1-29

Read the title and the first paragraph. Which of the following do you think the writer will talk about?

a. The rules that must be followed during the competitions
b. The history of water ballet
c. The number of people who participate today
d. The sport's rigorous demands
e. The training process in various countries
f. How traditional ballet and underwater ballet are similar
g. The ways in which the sport has changed over the years

# The *Beauty* and *Power* of WATER BALLET

1   Those who wish to succeed in water ballet will need the elegance of a ballerina and the strength of a long distance swimmer. Within its relatively short history, water ballet has captured the admiration of millions and has earned recognition as
5   a legitimate sport.

Water ballet has attracted fans since the early 1900s. Annette Kellerman, an Australian, is often credited as the founder of this sport. As a child, she was afflicted with rickets, a disease that weakens the bones. She began swimming in order to
10  strengthen her legs. After years of practice, she dubbed herself an "underwater ballerina" and started to perform a swimming and diving routine in a glass tank. Her act was so dazzling that she was soon convinced to take her show to America, where it had triumphant success.

15  Originally an individual sport, water ballet became a popular

group activity after membership in water ballet clubs grew. In the 1930s, it was renamed "synchronized swimming," which more accurately describes the perfect unison of swimmers' dance moves. It wasn't until the 1980s that it was
20 included in the Olympic Games as a competitive sport.

Today's synchronized swimmers are more athletic than the water ballerinas of the past. Members of the Aquamaids, the toughest synchronized swimming club in America, practice eight hours a day, six days a week. Not only do
25 they complete thousands of laps every week, they also spend numerous hours in gymnastics classes. Although it's a formidable commitment, joining the Aquamaids is the best choice for anyone who wants to make the US Olympic team. This club has produced more than 60 percent of the swimmers that have gone to the Olympics to participate in the sport.

30
There are other options available for professional synchronized swimmers. One of the most famous groups in the world is the Weeki Wachee Mermaids, who put on shows in Florida. These talented swimmers have been doing amazing stunts in an underwater theater for over 60 years.
35 Interestingly, the mermaid costumes are based on the original designs that were used by Annette Kellerman during her acts almost 100 years ago.

It's true that synchronized swimmers make their sport look effortless, but don't be fooled! It takes extensive training to
40 pull off the complicated movements these real-life mermaids perform every day.

# AFTER YOU READ

## A. Vocabulary

*Fill in the blanks with the word choices given. Change the word form if necessary.*

> dub / afflict / admiration / formidable / legitimate

1. Linda has great _____ for her father. She hopes to follow his example.

2. AIDS is a big problem in Africa. Millions of people are _____ with the fatal disease.

3. Jamaican sprinter Usain Bolt has been _____ the "Lightning Bolt" by the media.

4. At 8,848 meters, Mount Everest presents the most _____ climb in the world.

5. Some say that bowling isn't a _____ sport because bowlers don't use all of their muscles.

## B. Comprehension Check

*Match the two parts.*

1. Gracefulness and perseverance are _____.

2. Strengthening her poor health was _____.

3. Clubs became popular, so it was natural for _____.

4. Those who hope to make the US Olympic squad should join the Aquamaids _____.

5. The Weeki Wachee Mermaids continue to maintain _____.

a. some of the essence of Annette Kellerman

b. because the group is known for producing exceptional synchronized swimmers

c. necessary for becoming a water ballerina

d. Annette Kellerman's motivation to take up swimming

e. water ballet to evolve from a solo activity into a group sport

## C. Discussion

*Share your opinion with the class.*

In recent years, the Weeki Wachee Mermaids have become one of the only synchronized swimming groups to accept male swimmers. Today, male synchronized swimmers are not allowed to participate in most competitions, including the Olympics. Do you think men should receive equal opportunities in synchronized swimming?

# WRITING

Unit 7

## Spice Up Your Sentences

Dull sentences make a paragraph boring. Read the tips and choose the better sentence of each pair.

**Tip 1: Alternate sentence length.** Sentences can be combined for variety.

| | |
|---|---|
| _____ | Nick is passionate about playing basketball. He's proud to play for his school. |
| _____ | Nick is passionate about playing basketball and proudly represents his school. |

**Tip 2: Vary sentence openings.** Try not to repeat words, especially the, it, or this.

| | |
|---|---|
| _____ | Because the home team's lead was slim, their supporters were nervous. |
| _____ | The home team's lead was slim. The supporters were nervous. |

**Tip 3: Use expressive language.** Include more meaningful terminology.

| | |
|---|---|
| _____ | Nick's 12 points gave the team the momentum they needed to triumph during last Saturday's game. |
| _____ | Nick played well during the last game. |

**Tip 4: Avoid repetition.** Use synonyms or adjust the sentence structure.

| | |
|---|---|
| _____ | There were many spectators in the stands at the game. It was the final game of the season. |
| _____ | As it was the final game of the season, the stands were packed full of spectators. |

## Task

*Rewrite the following paragraph on a separate piece of paper. Spice up the sentences.*

Athletes often get bad injuries. Australian rugby player Ben Czislowski went to the doctor. He went because he had a headache for four months. The doctor saw another player's tooth stuck in Ben's forehead! This was why Ben had a headache. American speed skater J. R. Celski hurt himself. He did this by cutting his thigh with his skate blade. Baseball is bad, too. Most pitchers throw a ball at 70 to 80 miles per hour. It can cause severe damage to a batter if it hits him or her. Mike Piazza played for the New York Mets. Mike was hit in the head with a ball. The ball was going so fast that it shattered his helmet! Everyone should be careful when they play sports.

# EXTRA WRITING PRACTICE

## BEFORE YOU WRITE
*Rewrite the facts below about different national sports to make them more interesting.*

### United States – Baseball

The National Association of Base Ball Players was started in 1857. It is America's favorite sport.

  Ever since the National Association of Base
  Ball Players was founded in 1857, baseball
  has been a beloved pastime in America.

### Canada – Ice Hockey

Hockey began in Canada, but unfortunately, no one knows which city it began in.

_____

_____

(originate, birth, mystery)

### Scotland – Golf

Golf began in Scotland. Now Edinburgh has 21 golf courses.

_____

_____

(hail from, modern-day, boast)

### Japan – Sumo Wrestling

A sumo wrestler weighs about 400 pounds. That is very heavy!

_____

_____

(average weight, lightweight)

## WRITE IT UP
*Write a 150-word paragraph discussing the above national sports. Remember to spice up your sentences and include as many adjective clauses as you can.*

### CHERISHED NATIONAL PASTIMES

Sports have been uniting citizens in playful rivalry for hundreds of years!

_____

_____

_____

_____

_____

_____

_____

_____

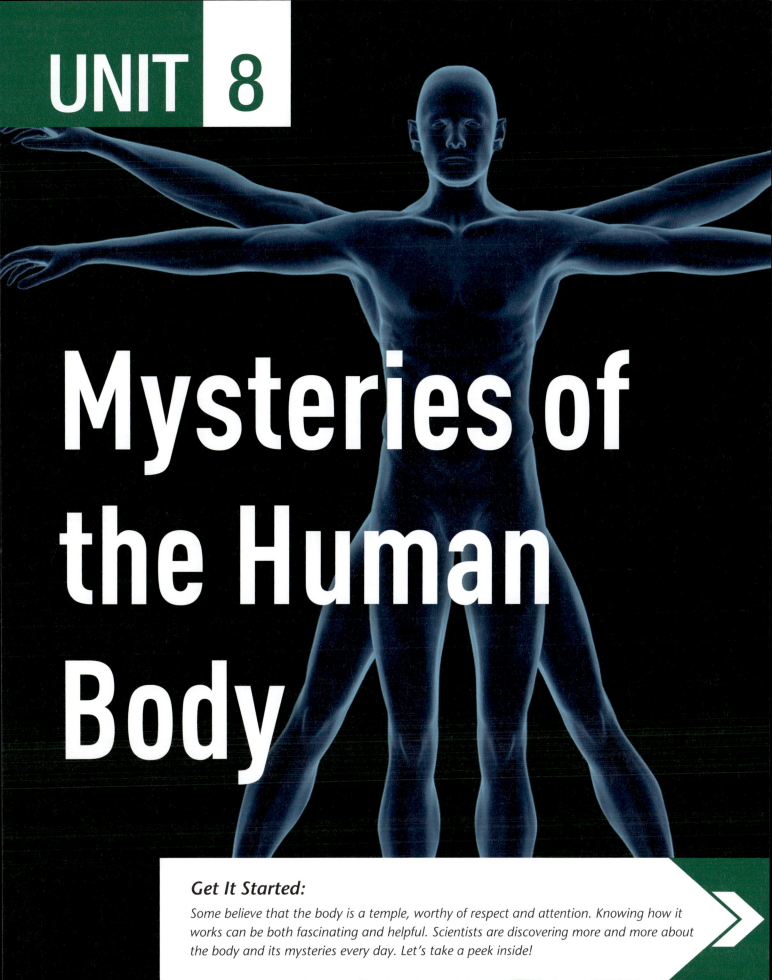

# UNIT 8

# Mysteries of the Human Body

**Get It Started:**
Some believe that the body is a temple, worthy of respect and attention. Knowing how it works can be both fascinating and helpful. Scientists are discovering more and more about the body and its mysteries every day. Let's take a peek inside!

# VOCABULARY

### Task 1
Match the following words with their correct definitions.  2-01

1. trauma _____
2. tissue _____
3. controversial _____
4. external _____
5. operational _____
6. transplant _____
7. phenomenon _____

a. working and ready to be used
b. something that happens or exists in society, science, or nature
c. severe injury
d. a collection of cells that form the different parts of humans, animals and plants
e. relating to the outside of a person's body
f. a medical operation in which a new organ is put into someone's body
g. causing disagreement or discussion

### Task 2
Learning root words can help expand your vocabulary. Fill in the correct forms.

| Verb | Noun | Adjective |
|---|---|---|
|  | organ, organism |  |
| digest |  |  |
| operate |  |  |
| purify |  |  |
| insulate |  |  |
| infect |  |  |

# LISTENING & SPEAKING

### A. Comprehension Check

Listen to the conversation and circle the answers.  2-02

1. Why does Lina want to begin studying right away?
   a. So they will finish ahead of schedule
   b. To cover as many topics as they can
   c. To outperform her study partner

2. How does Pete think organ printers will progress in the future?
   a. The principal purpose of the machines will greatly change.
   b. They'll be able to create both internal and external organs.
   c. They won't be mass-produced at all.

3. Why will organ printing become more important?
   a. There will be fewer eligible donors.
   b. The need for organ transplants will decrease in the future.
   c. The demand for new organs is soaring.

4. What does Lina think about organ printing?
   a. The technology will never be popular in the medical community.
   b. Although the idea is still in its infancy, it will be widely used soon.
   c. It has lower risks than traditional transplant operations.

B. **Partial Dictation**

Listen again and fill in the blanks.  2-02

# Organ Printing

*Medical students Pete and Lina are in a coffee shop, preparing for their exam.*

**Pete:** Ready to get down to business?

**Lina:** If we study hard now, maybe we can knock off early. Deal?

**Pete:** Deal. Let's review the lesson on organ printing.

**Lina:** Yes. Creating fully functional 1. _____ with a machine sounds like a myth, but it's a reality!

**Pete:** Do you remember how this type of machine works?

**Lina:** Professor Stratman 2. _____ the process to how a printer copies documents.

**Pete:** Oh, right. The machine scans an image of the organ, and 3. _____ from the patient is fed into it. A new organ then grows from the tissue.

**Lina:** Yeah. Although more work still needs to be done, it certainly isn't a pipe dream anymore. It's believed that it will take about 50 years before doctors can rely on these printers. Until then, human donors will 4. _____ the machines' production.

**Pete:** In the future, the printers will also be able to produce 5. _____ organs, like printing skin directly onto a patient.

**Lina:** Did the professor say whether or not this is 6. _____? It seems like progressive science is often met with opposition.

**Pete:** Since the benefits are so numerous, it's difficult to find fault with it. With the demand for 7. _____ on the rise in the last 10 years, doctors can utilize the technology to make organs accessible to needy patients, like the elderly or trauma victims.

**Lina:** That's right. Once these are 8. _____, I'm sure they'll become an everyday medical phenomenon.

**knock off:**
to stop working and go somewhere else

**pipe dream:**
an idea or plan that is impossible

**be met with:**
to experience something, usually something unpleasant

**Practice the conversation with your partner.**

# LANGUAGE FOCUS

Talking About Work
Discussing Fantasy

## Talking About Work

| Getting Started | Finishing Up |
|---|---|
| • get down to business<br>• get cracking<br>• hop to it | • knock off<br>• call it a day<br>• pack it in |

### Task 1

*Fill in the underlined blanks with the appropriate expressions above and then match the two parts.*

1. An executive meeting was called in order to _____.
2. When the students were ready to _____.
3. Everyone wanted to _____, _____.

a. but employees were required to stay until the final customer left the store
b. _____ on the company's new project
c. _____, the professor handed out the exam papers

## Discussing Fantasy

• a pipe dream   • pie in the sky   • wishful thinking
• a flight of fancy   • a castle in the air

### Task 2

*Use the expressions above to complete the short dialogs.*
*Do not use the same expressions twice.*

1. **A:** I want to open my own tailoring business even though I think it's just _____.
   **B:** You would make a great tailor. That's not _____ !

2. **A:** It sounds like _____ that a new subway line could be built within six months.
   **B:** I know. I don't think the mayor's _____ will ever come true.

# GRAMMAR | Adverb Clauses

Unit 8

An adverb clause contains a subject and a verb and is usually introduced by a subordinating conjunction.

## Basic Types

| Type | Signal Words | Example |
|------|--------------|---------|
| place | where, wherever | **Wherever** she went in the house, she was reminded of the events she had held there. |
| time | after, before, until, while, once | It will take about 50 years **before** doctors can rely on these printers. |
| cause | because, since, as | **Since** the benefits are so numerous, it's difficult to find fault with it. |
| purpose | so (that), in order that | Please confirm your attendance early **so** no one will be left behind on the day of the outing. |
| contrast | while, although, even though | **Although** more work still needs to be done, it certainly isn't a pipe dream anymore. |
| condition | if, unless | **If** we study hard now, maybe we can knock off early. |

## Reduced Form

| Rule | Example |
|------|---------|
| 1. Drop the subject and the be verb. | **While** he was trekking across the mountains, Dale almost stepped on a snake. |
| 2. Drop the subject and change the main verb to the -ing form. | **Although** he felt [**feeling**] rather sick, the professor managed to finish his speech. |
| 3. **Because** can sometimes be omitted when the subject is dropped and the main verb is changed to the -ing form. | Because she is [**Being**] a superficial person, Kitty cares more about money than love. |
| 4. If the subjects are different, do not use the reduced form. | Virginia waited inside the cabin **until** it stopped raining. |

## Task

*Match the two parts and fill in the underlined blanks with these subordinators:* **until, even though, once, if, because.**

1. _____ the koala is often called the koala "bear," _____.

2. All passengers should remain seated with their seat belts fastened _____.

3. You can't convict a person of murder _____.

4. _____ a person has been accepted to a prestigious university, _____.

5. It is impossible to outrun Greg _____.

a. _____ he has received extensive marathon training

b. it is actually a pouched mammal, like the kangaroo

c. his or her chances of having a successful career are higher

d. _____ there is no concrete evidence

e. _____ the airplane has come to a complete stop

83

# READING

## BEFORE YOU READ  2-03

*You are going to see the following phrases in the article. What do the underlined words mean? Look them up in a dictionary and explain their meanings to your partner in English.*

mental <u>feats</u> / developmental <u>disorder</u> / <u>aptitude</u> for music /
<u>severe</u> brain damage / <u>unbelievable</u> calculations / <u>mysterious</u> organ

*Now select the questions you think the author will answer.*

a. What are some unusual side effects of severe brain injuries?
b. Can all people with an aptitude for music do fast calculations?
c. Why will the body's most mysterious organ never be fully understood?
d. What questions are most commonly discussed by doctors regarding the brain?
e. What are some surprising talents that people with disorders have?

# Disabilities and Genius

1   Even after years of being studied, the brain continues to hold many secrets. One mystery is why some people who struggle to complete simple tasks are able to perform mental feats that would challenge even the most intelligent. These individuals may hold the key to
5   discovering how the brain can be trained to work at its best.

   Ellen Boudreaux was blind by four months old and was later diagnosed with autism, a developmental disorder. It took her until the age of four to learn how to walk. Soon after, she taught herself to determine where obstacles are by making
10  sounds as she moves. Doctors postulate that her amazing sense of hearing combined with the sounds she makes create a type of sonar, like what bats use to fly at night. Her extraordinary hearing has also given her an aptitude for

84

music. By using her ability to recognize different tones, she has mastered several instruments. She can recall any song that she hears and then play it perfectly.

When Kim Peek was born, he had such severe brain damage that it was believed he could never live independently. This ended up being partly true. While he was alive, Kim had difficulty with physical movements, such as buttoning his shirt; however, he had reading powers that can only be described as miraculous. When Kim read, he read one page with his left eye and one with his right eye. What's even more impressive is that he could remember everything he read. He could recall the content of at least 12,000 books from memory!

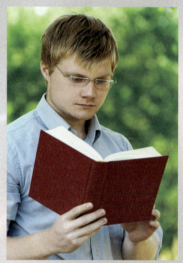

Although he wasn't diagnosed with autism until the age of 25, Daniel Tammet started showing signs of remarkable genius after a series of childhood seizures. Daniel can relate colors, shapes, and textures to every number. To him, these figures look like beautiful landscapes, which makes it easy for him to do unbelievable calculations in his head. He claims that 333 is the most attractive number. Additionally, Daniel can learn languages with bewildering ease. Once, Daniel was challenged to learn a language in a week. He learned the language so well that a native speaker successfully interviewed him at the end of the week.

These geniuses are examples of why the brain is such a mysterious organ. If scientists can find the reasons behind the vast variations in mental abilities, they will achieve great things in the future.

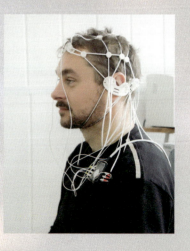

# AFTER YOU READ

## A. Vocabulary

*Fill in the blanks with the word choices given. Change the word form if necessary.*

> postulate / bewildering / variation / diagnose / miraculous

1. She was _____ with breast cancer, but fortunately it was discovered at an early stage.

2. The illusionist made a _____ underwater escape from a locked box.

3. It has been _____ that a person's height is an inherited trait.

4. The number of choices Janet was presented with was _____, so she couldn't make a decision.

5. There are countless _____ in the appearance of different dog breeds.

## B. Comprehension Check

*Circle the answers.*

1. What is the reason for Ellen's fantastic musical abilities?
   a. She learned music to fight off boredom.
   b. She can hear individual sounds distinctly.
   c. Her parents are celebrated musicians.
   d. She knows how far sounds travel.

2. What is NOT said about Kim?
   a. He could read two pages simultaneously.
   b. He was unable to fasten his clothing.
   c. It was easier for him to memorize facts that he found fascinating.
   d. Kim could answer perplexing questions about things he had read.

3. Why is Daniel able to do complicated calculations so easily?
   a. Daniel's brain perceives a link between numbers and other elements.
   b. He has memorized thousands of calculations, so he recalls them easily.
   c. The answers come to him during seizures.
   d. He relates numbers to different sounds.

4. Which of the following statements is true?
   a. Only people that have extreme difficulties will excel at certain tasks.
   b. For a brain to function abnormally, it must be damaged in early childhood.
   c. It won't be long before the mysteries of the brain are solved.
   d. Research still needs to be done to discover the brain's full potential.

## C. Discussion

*Share your opinion with the class.*

> Helen Keller was struck deaf and blind after falling ill as a child. Despite this, she learned to speak and "hear" by touching others' lips as they spoke and later became a motivational speaker. Whom do you consider more talented: someone who is born with impressive natural abilities or someone who works hard to reach their goals? Do you know any related inspirational stories?

# WRITING

## The Descriptive Essay

A descriptive essay uses specific details and figurative language to create a vivid picture for readers.

### Guidelines

☑ Imagine your subject and note any details that come to mind.
☑ Depict how your subject looks, feels, smells, sounds, or tastes.
☑ When describing people, portray their appearance and actions.

### Figurative Language

Figurative language animates written descriptions. Here are the most common types:

| Simile | The girl looked as delicate as a flower. |
|---|---|
| Metaphor | The lake's surface is a shining mirror. |

## Task

*Read the passage. Write the descriptions of each subject in the chart below.*

Conjoined twins are twins whose bodies are fused together during pregnancy. The world's longest surviving pair is George and Lori Schappell. Born in 1961, they are joined at the head.

Despite this, they have personalities that are as distinct as night and day. George is an outgoing musician and has won an L.A. Music Award for Best New Country Artist. Lori, on the other hand, is more reserved. She tries to make herself "invisible" during George's performances. She does, however, love to go bowling. They have their own bedrooms, which they decorate very differently. Music posters liven up George's room, while Lori's has a more feminine feel. They've even acted in an episode of *Nip/Tuck*. They are determined to not let their situation hinder them from accomplishing great things.

| George and Lori | George | Lori |
|---|---|---|
|  |  |  |

# EXTRA WRITING PRACTICE

## BEFORE YOU WRITE
*Match the words or phrases in bold on the left to the more descriptive terms on the right.*

- keep skin **looking nice** • • radiant
- sun rays can **damage** skin • • as smooth as a baby's cheeks
- smoking **is harmful for** skin • • strip away
- toxic chemicals **remove** protective oils • • fry
- skin feels **good** • • suffocates

## WRITE IT UP
*Write a 150-word descriptive essay about skin care. Use descriptive and figurative language. Also include some adverb clauses and the phrases from the section above.*

**Title:** _____ (Be creative.)

**Introduction:** Get readers' attention. → Most people are ignorant about the necessity of skin care.

**Body:** Detail skin care methods and include an example of someone with beautiful skin. →

**Conclusion:** Use a clincher. →

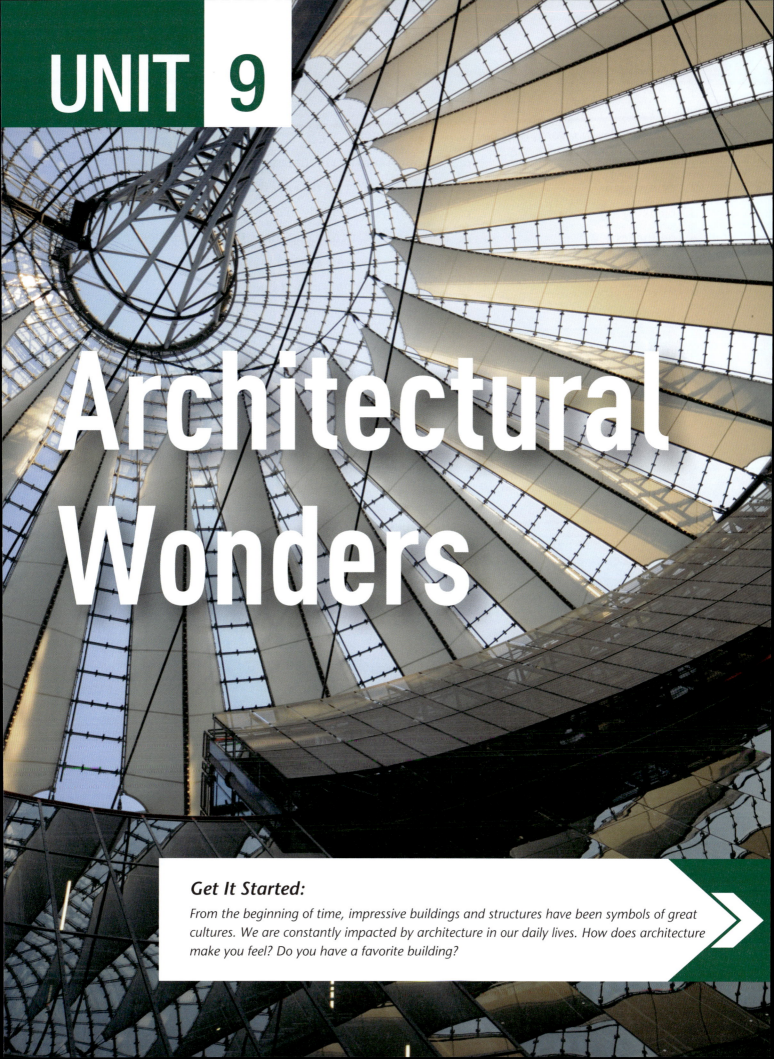

# UNIT 9

# Architectural Wonders

### Get It Started:
From the beginning of time, impressive buildings and structures have been symbols of great cultures. We are constantly impacted by architecture in our daily lives. How does architecture make you feel? Do you have a favorite building?

# VOCABULARY

## Task 1

*Match the following words with their correct definitions.* 🎧 2-04

1. candidate _____
2. extravagant _____
3. bleak _____
4. aesthetics _____
5. awe-inspiring _____
6. architecture _____
7. influence _____

a. causing you to feel great respect
b. to have an effect on the way that someone behaves or thinks
c. something that is likely to experience something
d. cold and without any pleasant or comfortable features
e. the study of beauty, especially beauty in art
f. the design and style of buildings
g. spending too much money

## Task 2

*Finish the description with the words provided.*

inspiration / characterized / landmark / staggering / carvings / symbolic

**Brief Description**

**Name:**
Forbidden City
**Location:**
Beijing, China 🇨🇳
**Dates Built:**
1406–1420

The architects responsible for this palace complex focused on horizontal design elements. Thus, the buildings are ❶_____ by solid platforms and thick roofs. The roofs are covered with yellow tiles, as the color was ❷_____ of imperial power.

**Brief Description**

**Name:**
Arch of Titus
**Location:**
Rome, Italy 🇮🇹
**Date Erected:**
81 AD

This monument to the Roman emperor Titus is ❸_____ in size. The giant arch measures 13.50 meters wide, 15.40 meters high, and 4.75 meters deep. On the inside walls, there are ❹_____ showing the victory parade when the emperor returned to Rome from war. The distinct design is the ❺_____ for the Arc de Triomphe, a famous ❻_____ in Paris, France.

# LISTENING & SPEAKING

## A. Comprehension Check

*Listen to the conversation and check **T** if the statement is true, **F** if it's false.* 🎧 2-05

1. T ☐ F ☐ Somehow Christy feels unhappy and depressed at school.
2. T ☐ F ☐ Carrie thinks Christy's mood is being affected by her surroundings.
3. T ☐ F ☐ Carrie has been studying the effects of color for years.
4. T ☐ F ☐ Carrie believes that specific shapes can change the way you feel.
5. T ☐ F ☐ Christy finds contemporary architecture dull and boring.

**B. Partial Dictation**

*Listen again and fill in the blanks.* 2-05

Unit 9

# Emotions and Architecture

*Christy comes home and is greeted by her sister, Carrie.*

**Carrie:** Hey, you look tired. What's got you down in the mouth?

**Christy:** I've had it with school. I don't have any difficult **1.** _____, but I feel weighed down and depressed.

**Carrie:** That could be because of **2.** _____. Some elements of contemporary design can make you feel gloomy.

**Christy:** That sounds like a fish story.

**Carrie:** Well, according to scientists, the aesthetics of a space are what really influence a person's mood.

**Christy:** All right. So how do design features **3.** _____ whether I feel at ease?

**Carrie:** Color is one factor. Studies have shown that red causes better task **4.** _____, while cool colors make us less energetic. And it's angles that can make fearful emotions soar. The **5.** _____ for this is that in nature, angles suggest something to avoid—a sharp rock or the edge of a cliff.

**Christy:** I see. Too many architectural angles make us feel on edge. But out of all the styles of architecture, it's modern design that I'm a fan of. It removes all those **6.** _____ extras.

**Carrie:** Maybe you just haven't noticed the effects today's architecture has on you. I haven't been to your school recently, but it's pretty **7.** _____, right?

**Christy:** Yeah. The building is rectangular, constructed out of concrete, and painted white. There's nothing awe-inspiring about it.

**Carrie:** Seems like a good **8.** _____ for reconstruction.

**Christy:** Oh yes. I'm sure the school will sign off on that.

**down in the mouth:**
depressed

**have had it:**
to be extremely tired

**weighed down:**
unhappy and worried

**fish story:**
a great big lie

**at ease:**
relaxed

**on edge:**
nervous

**sign off on:**
to support

**Practice the conversation with your partner.**

91

# LANGUAGE FOCUS — Feeling Down / Expressing Stress and Comfort

**Feeling Down**

- be down in the mouth
- be down in the dumps
- be in low spirits
- feel sick at heart
- feel blue/low

## Task 1

Listen to the audio. Check which tips Rosie agrees to.  2-06

### 5 Steps to Lift Your Low Spirit!

- ☐ **Exercise!** You may feel too blue to run on the treadmill or lift weights, but it'll help you beat depression.
- ☐ **Create a cheerful atmosphere.** Brightening up your living space can brighten up your life!
- ☐ **Put on some lively tunes.** Listening to pop music will have your toes tapping in no time.
- ☐ **Make yourself look stunning!** Discard all of your sloppy outfits.
- ☐ **Go party!** Friends can bring you up whenever you're down in the dumps.

**Expressing Stress and Comfort**

| Feeling Stressed | Feeling Comfortable |
|---|---|
| • have had it (with *something/someone*) | • feel/be at ease |
| • feel weighed down | • breathe easy |
| • have (*one's*) hands full | • be without a care in the world |

## Task 2

Fill in the blanks with the appropriate expressions.

1. I can't finish that assignment in time unless I come into the office on Saturday. I have _____!

2. She seems _____ by work. She won't be able to _____ until the weekend.

3. The service at the five-star restaurant was fabulous, and the waiter really made us _____.

# GRAMMAR | Cleft Sentences

Unit 9

Cleft structures are useful for placing emphasis on a certain part of a sentence.

## Preparatory *It* and *What* Clauses

|  | Basic Sentence | Cleft Sentence |
|---|---|---|
| it | Christy has been a fan of modern design since she started university. | • **It is modern design that** Christy has been a fan of since she started university.<br>• **It is Christy who** has been a fan of modern design since she started university. |
| what | I've had it with school. | **What** I've had it with is school. |

## Reduced Form

| Focus | Basic Sentence | Cleft Sentence |
|---|---|---|
| person | Matt dressed up as a gypsy for Halloween. | **The person who** dressed up as a gypsy for Halloween **was** Matt. |
| place | Heather wants to eat snacks at the night market. | **The place where** Heather wants to eat snacks **is** the night market. |
| time | Thomas Jefferson died on July 4, 1826. | **The day (when)** Thomas Jefferson died **was** July 4, 1826. |
| reason | Ken dropped by the bank to make a deposit. | **The reason** Ken dropped by the bank **was** to make a deposit. |
| action | The pedestrian waited for the light to change. | **What** the pedestrian **did was** wait for the light to change. |
| a whole sentence | The flight was postponed because of a heavy snowstorm. | **What** happened **was that** the flight was postponed because of a heavy snowstorm. |

## Task 1

*Match the two parts.*

1. What is thought of as the most difficult aspect of learning to swim _____.

2. According to the news report, it was a lit cigarette that _____.

3. The place where we put the trophies _____.

4. What I would prefer to do first is _____.

5. Although I know I need to diet, it is my girlfriend _____.

a. is in the main lobby, near the principal's office

b. is taking the first plunge

c. to visit the exhibition on the top floor of this building

d. that nags me about my weight all the time

e. sparked the massive forest fire

## Task 2

*Rewrite the sentences into the cleft structure using the words provided.*

ex. The doctor just needs a couple of minutes to fill out your prescription. **(all)**

→ All the doctor needs is a couple of minutes to fill out your prescription.

1. The speaker said something totally unacceptable. **(what)**

→ _____

2. Mary initiated the campaign in order to raise funds for the children's hospital. **(reason)**

→ _____

93

# READING

## BEFORE YOU READ  2-07

Look at the pictures and captions. What do you think the reading will be about?

a. How the designs of office buildings have evolved over the years
b. Using bizarre building materials in modern architecture
c. Examples of remarkable structures that use interesting designs
d. How modern offices meet international standards

# Who Says Buildings Have to Be Boring?

1   From the unusual to the practical, modern architecture has countless styles. All across the globe, what many architects are doing is pushing the envelope when it comes to creating buildings that fulfill the needs of leading enterprises.

### Vodafone Headquarters

5   When Vodafone announced a contest to design its headquarters in Portugal, the cell phone giant probably didn't expect to receive the plans from the architectural firm Barbosa & Guimarães. It was Vodafone's slogan, "Life in Motion," that these
10  architects used as their inspiration. The building appears to be moving! Both the exterior and the interior of the building are full of geometric patterns. The designers were only able to achieve this look because of concrete—it can be shaped into any
15  imaginable form. The completed structure is so awe-inspiring that it has won numerous awards.

By constructing Vodafone's headquarters out of a material that is easily molded, the architects have created a symbol of abstract design.
Photo: Flickr / LeonL

## The Basket Building

Some architecture can best be described as playful. These types of structures often fall into the category of novelty designs, in which buildings resemble the merchandise that its company sells. The Longaberger Company's Home Office in Newark, Ohio, is one such example. This seven-story headquarters is a dead ringer for the company's biggest seller: the Longaberger Medium Market Basket. The design was the invention of its founder, Dave Longaberger. As he was known to be a joker, many people thought he was kidding when he announced his plans, but his funny suggestion increased publicity for the business.

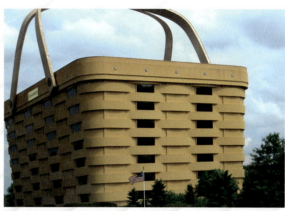

Shaped like a giant gift basket, the Basket Building is a great example of how architecture can be both useful and entertaining. Photo: Flickr / ellenm1

## The More London Development

As environmental protection has become part of global consciousness, the world's foremost architects are trying to come up with the most prestigious green building. Once construction of 7 More London was finished, Foster + Partners had successfully created the most eco-friendly building in London. It is the first structure in the capital city to receive an OUTSTANDING rating from the country's green building ranking organization. The More London development consists of several buildings and is home to London's City Hall, as well as various cafés, shops, and an open-air area full of sculptures and water fountains. Foster + Partners is responsible for the look of the entire complex, and the company is well-known for using glass and steel to design amazing architecture all over the world.

The unusual shape of London's City Hall is not only a stunning design, but it also helps save the planet. Solar panels were installed to reduce the emissions of the building by 3,000 tons. Photo: Flickr / Elias.gomez

If you're an architecture enthusiast, there are plenty of notable buildings that are sure to thrill you. Each year, the field of architecture moves in interesting directions thanks to architects' ingenuity.

# AFTER YOU READ

## A. Vocabulary

*Fill in the blanks with the word choices given. Change the word form if necessary.*

| uniqueness / exposure / pioneer / addicted / identical |
|---|

1. The company was determined to push the envelope in its industry. It _____ a cutting-edge method of production.

2. When tablet computers were first released, many considered them a novelty. Now, however, their _____ is no longer surprising.

3. Joe was a dead ringer for a famous news anchor. In fact, they looked _____, so he was often mistaken for the celebrity.

4. Organizers put a lot of effort into the event's publicity. Thanks to the _____, the attendance was greater than expected.

5. Bob is a big baseball enthusiast. Sometimes his wife thinks he is too _____ to the game.

## B. Comprehension Check

*Match the two parts.*

1. The idea behind Vodafone's slogan motivated _____.

2. When an architect wants more flexibility in his or her design, _____.

3. Surprisingly, it was originally the founder's idea _____.

4. According to the most recent rankings, _____.

5. Since environmental issues are generating concern worldwide, _____.

a. for the headquarters to resemble the company's merchandise

b. 7 More London causes less carbon emissions than any other office building

c. concrete is the perfect material to use because it can be shaped easily

d. green buildings have been gaining popularity in recent years

e. the architects who came up with the innovative design plans

## C. Discussion

*Share your opinion with the class.*

Can you name a few of the nations that are known for their architectural inventiveness? What about your country? Which landmark in your city has the most celebrated design? Do you know if there is an interesting story behind its style?

# WRITING

## Add Emphasis to Sentences

**DO**
- 😊 Repeat important words in a series.
- 😊 Use cleft sentences.
- 😊 Ask a question after a statement.

**DON'T**
- 😞 Boldface, underline, or repeatedly italicize words.
- 😞 Use capital letters.
- 😞 Include multiple exclamation points.

### Emphasis Transition Words

definitely, extremely, obviously, certainly, in fact, surprisingly, always, never, without a doubt, particularly, in any case, above all . . .

## Task 1

*Underline the stressed points in the paragraph below and circle any emphasis words.*

When British immigrants settled in northeast America, they brought their architectural traditions. Not surprisingly, intact historical buildings from this era feature a simpler version of British style, as importing material was costly. Building materials were chosen for their easy production: wood, brick, and stone. Certainly, the most prized decorative element of any house was the chimney. Before this invention, it was only through the windows that smoke from fires could be ventilated. Can you imagine what a relief it was to no longer have smoke polluting the house? Modern architects continue to build homes in this colonial style, especially in New England.

## Task 2

*Rewrite the paragraph to make it more emphatic on a separate sheet of paper.*

Suburbs are common, and they can be found ALL OVER the United States. The federal government offered loans and made home ownership affordable after World War II ended. The existence of cars enabled people to drive away from the city to other neighborhoods. The preference for private homes made them popular. The availability of land made it possible for them to be built. So, suburban areas were created. Supporters believe suburbs are better for families. Others argue building them is bad for the environment. Suburbs are popular!!!!!!

# EXTRA WRITING PRACTICE

## BEFORE YOU WRITE
*Do some Internet research on these buildings. Write down interesting facts using the suggested vocabulary words for emphasis.*

**OLDEST**

### Megalithic Temples

**Location:** Malta
**Built:** 4,000–2,000 BC

remarkable, immense, detailed

- These remarkable structures were built between 4,000 and 2,000 BC.
- Their courtyards are immense.
- Their outer walls are decorated with detailed carvings.

Photo: Flickr / Neil and Kathy Carey

**LARGEST**

### Boeing Everett Factory

**Location:** Everett, Washington
**Covers:** 98.3 acres

extraordinary, impressive, spacious

Photo: Flickr / prayitno

**MOST EXPENSIVE**

### Wynn Las Vegas

**Location:** Las Vegas Strip in Paradise, Nevada
**Cost:** $2.7 billion

breathtaking, glittery, staggering

Photo: Flickr / xiquinhosilva

## WRITE IT UP
*Write a 150-word paragraph about the buildings above. Emphasize the characteristic that makes each famous—age, size, and cost. Include two cleft sentences.*

### Amazing Constructions

There are special architectures that are sure to leave visitors to them in awe. Take the Megalithic Temples of Malta, for example.

# UNIT 10

# Loving the Earth

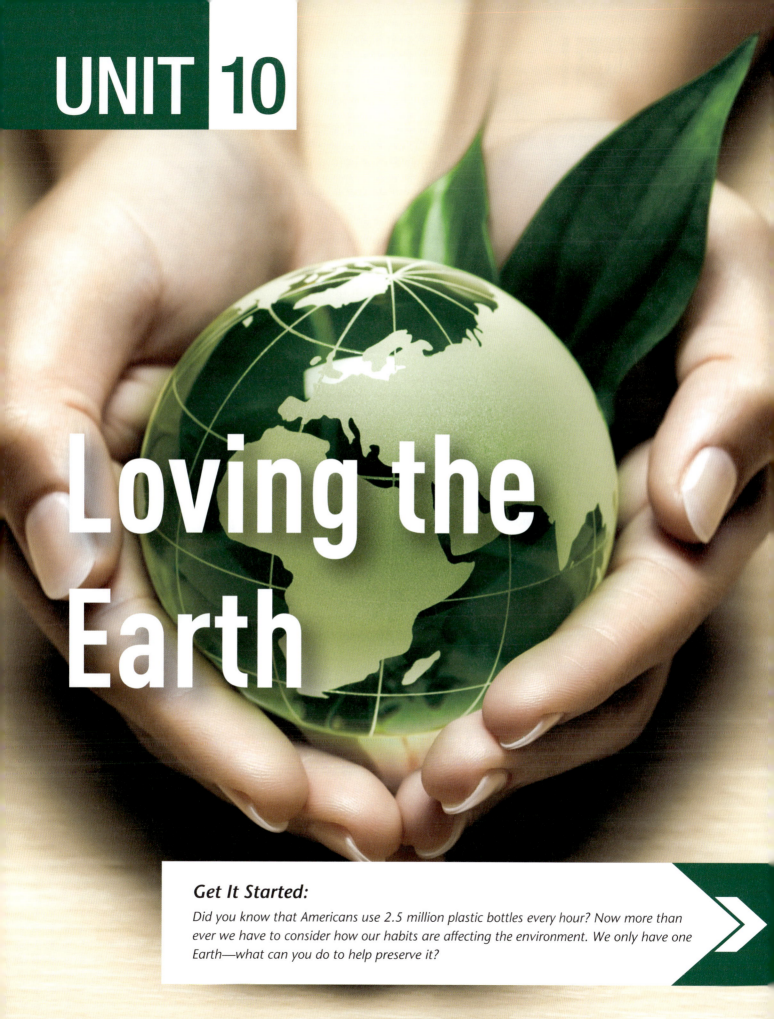

### Get It Started:
Did you know that Americans use 2.5 million plastic bottles every hour? Now more than ever we have to consider how our habits are affecting the environment. We only have one Earth—what can you do to help preserve it?

# VOCABULARY

## Task 1

*Match the following words with their correct definitions.*  🔊 2-08

1. dumpster _____
2. convert _____
3. initiate _____
4. discard _____
5. innovative _____
6. emission _____
7. conservation _____

a. using new methods or ideas
b. to cause something to begin
c. a large metal container used for waste
d. to throw away
e. the act of sending out gas, heat, light, etc.
f. the protection of nature
g. to change something into something else

## Task 2

*Fill in the blanks with the word choices given.*

deteriorating / alternative / susceptible / climate / agriculture / disappear

### World Wildlife Fund
### Memorandum

**Introduction:** As the Amazon rainforest is quickly ❶ _____,
40 percent of it could ❷ _____ by 2030.
The other problem that must be eliminated is ❸ _____
change damage to the ❹ _____ sector. Farmers are
choosing to grow fruit that is less ❺ _____ to the warmer
temperatures. We should send a team to teach ❻ _____
farming practices as soon as possible.

# LISTENING & SPEAKING

### A. Comprehension Check

*Listen to the conversation and check **T** if the statement is true, **F** if it's false.*  🔊 2-09

1. T ☐ F ☐ Tim believes his school may have discarded items that could be reused in creative ways.

2. T ☐ F ☐ Old Navy stores donated flip-flops to organizations that maintain playgrounds.

3. T ☐ F ☐ Old Navy and TerraCycle cooperated on an environmental project.

4. T ☐ F ☐ TerraCycle makes money by recycling items that are normally thought to be unrecyclable.

5. T ☐ F ☐ Gum is made from rubber and can be transformed into plastic.

100

B. **Partial Dictation**

Listen again and fill in the blanks.  2-09

# Turning Trash into Treasure

*Tim and Linda walk out of class together.*

Tim: Hey, do you want to go dumpster diving with me after school?

Linda: Uhh, come again?

Tim: I'm going to root around in the school's dumpsters to find 1. _____.

root around: to search for something

Linda: Don't they already recycle?

Tim: I'm not talking about common recyclables, like plastics and glass. Consumers, thinking they're through using their old stuff, dispose of items that could be reused. If you unleash your creativity on old jeans, they can be 2. _____ into pot holders or book covers.

unleash: let loose

Linda: What an interesting notion! It actually sounds similar to something the chain clothing store Old Navy was doing. The company 3. _____ worn flip-flops and used the rubber as building material for playgrounds.

flip-flop: a type of open shoe, with a strap that goes between the big toe and the toe next to it

Tim: I know about that 4. _____ idea. In fact, Old Navy initiated the program in cooperation with a company called TerraCycle. Following its slogan "Eliminate the Idea of Waste," TerraCycle succeeds in turning the world's 5. _____ into a cash cow.

cash cow: a moneymaker

Linda: How can a company profit from trash?

Tim: The owner really knows the ins and outs of recycling. For example, TerraCycle transforms 6. _____ chewing gum into a variety of plastic products. Gum is essentially flavored plastic, so it's simple.

the ins and outs: the detailed facts of something

Linda: Sick. I'm never chewing gum again.

Tim: It's just going the extra mile for resource 7. _____. The less waste that's buried or burned, the more land that's available to use. It also reduces the amount of 8. _____ in the atmosphere.

go the extra mile: to try a little harder in order to achieve something

Linda: Wow. I guess one man's trash is another man's treasure.

**Practice the conversation with your partner.**

# LANGUAGE FOCUS

Searching Thoroughly
Talking About Experts

## Searching Thoroughly

- root around in (*something/a place*)
- turn (*a place*) inside out
- look high and low
- rifle through (*something*)
- go through (*something/a place*) with a fine-tooth comb

## Task 1

*Fill in the appropriate expressions. Some blanks may have more than one possible answer.*

1. The receptionist _____ her desk until she found the file folder.

2. After _____ his daughter's room _____, he realized that her bracelet was probably in the bathroom.

3. Despite _____ at the crime scene, the police failed to find any evidence.

## Talking About Experts

| know | the ins and outs of (*something*) <br> (*something*) inside out <br> (*something*) backwards and forwards |
|------|---|
| be | on the ball <br> up to speed |

## Task 2

*Rewrite the parts in bold to include the phrases above. There may be more than one possible answer.*

1. Jim **can always figure out what is wrong with computers**.

   → Jim _____.

2. Surgeons have to be **knowledgeable** to provide their patients with the best care possible.

   → Surgeons have to be _____ to provide their patients with the best care possible.

3. George **was well-informed about** how the vacuum cleaner worked.

   → George _____ how the vacuum cleaner worked.

# GRAMMAR

## Participles
## Participial Phrases

### Participles

A participle is a verb form which can be used as an adjective to modify a noun. It often ends in –ing or –ed.

| present participle (–ing) | • Turning old jeans into pot holders or book covers is an **interesting** notion.<br>• The **crying** baby seemed to have a fever. |
|---|---|
| past participle (–ed) | • The company collected **worn** flip-flops and used the rubber as building material for playgrounds.<br>• TerraCycle transforms **discarded** chewing gum into a variety of plastic products. |

### Participial Phrases

| Placement | Use | Examples |
|---|---|---|
| beginning | These come right before the nouns they describe and are followed by commas. | • **Following its slogan "Eliminate the Idea of Waste,"** TerraCycle succeeds in turning the world's garbage into a cash cow.<br>• **Annoyed by the noise from next door**, the guest requested to change rooms. |
| middle | If the information is important to the meaning of the sentence, the pattern doesn't use commas. | • Consumers, **thinking they're through using their old stuff**, dispose of items that could be reused.<br>• A group **angered by the new law** began holding protests downtown. |
| end | These usually come after the noun they describe. | • Old Navy initiated the program in cooperation with a company **called TerraCycle**.<br>• Glenda saw her classmate **running down the alley**. |

### Task

*Fill in the blanks using participial phrases.*

ex. The man always wears a gray jacket. He lives upstairs from me.

The man ___*always wearing a gray jacket*___ lives upstairs from me.

1. Megan hurried over to assist the victims. She had witnessed the accident only seconds before.

   _____, Megan hurried over to assist the victims.

2. The house was built upon a cliff. The cliff was surrounded by the ocean.

   The house was built upon a cliff _____.

3. The salesperson stared at Josh. She also tapped her finger impatiently.

   The salesperson, _____, stared at Josh.

4. Arkansas is known as the Natural State. It's considered one of the most scenic states in America.

   _____, Arkansas is considered one of the most scenic states in America.

## READING

**BEFORE YOU READ** 2-10

*Look at the title of the article. Select what you think overfishing refers to. There are multiple correct answers.*

a. Fish are caught before they are fully grown.
b. Eating fish that are too high in protein can have serious effects.
c. So many adult fish are harvested that there are not enough left to reproduce.
d. When fishing is done irresponsibly, it endangers wildlife.
e. Fishing provides a great food source for developing countries.

# OVERFISHING: The Enemy of Ocean Life

1   Today, the biggest threat to marine life is overfishing. Scientists predict that unsustainable fishing practices will cause the world's seafood supply to run out by 2048. Only through deliberate measures can this disaster be avoided.

5   Over three quarters of the Earth's surface is covered by water, yet many underwater species are becoming increasingly rare. The Food and Agriculture Organization of the United Nations estimates that more than 70 percent of the world's fish stocks have reached dangerously low numbers or are already depleted. This is due to a phenomenon called biological overfishing, which comes in three forms: growth, recruit,
10   and ecosystem. Growth overfishing occurs when fish are harvested before becoming mature. Because of the smaller size of the young fish, fishermen have to catch more to achieve their goal weight. Moreover,

when too many adult fish are caught, the reproduction of the species is likewise threatened; this is referred to as recruit overfishing. The third kind is perhaps the worst: ecosystem overfishing. In extreme cases, fishing changes a region's entire wildlife distribution. For example, poisonous jellyfish have experienced a recent population explosion in some oceans because they no longer face competition from predators.

Overfishing has severe consequences for humans, too. In Africa, the decline of fish known for eating disease-causing insects has been linked to an increased incidence of illness. There are also economical disadvantages, like those seen in Newfoundland, Canada. Cod fishing was the main trade in this province, but in 1992, fleets went to sea and returned empty-handed. The cod had vanished. Decades of overfishing resulted in their disappearance, and 40,000 people lost their source of income. Today, many communities are still struggling to recover.

If the industry acts now, the world's sea life can be saved. First, every fishery must limit the total number of fish caught, giving adults time to breed. Second, certain areas need to be protected, such as delicate sea floor habitats and coral reefs. Governments should work together to make dangerous fishing practices illegal. Consumers can make a difference, too, with just a little extra effort. Buy fish only from providers who practice sustainable fishing methods and never eat endangered species.

Oceans and lakes are filled with fascinating life forms that have existed for millions of years. Let's not allow our appetites to destroy them!

# AFTER YOU READ

## A. Vocabulary

*Fill in the blanks with the word choices given. Change the word form if necessary.*

> marine / reproduction / sustainable / incidence / deliberate

1. Consumers want to know where their food comes from to ensure that its continued production is _____.

2. The area of the sea near the east coast is famous for its diverse _____ life.

3. The police discovered that the bombing was _____ rather than accidental.

4. Although bulldog _____ can occur naturally, most females cannot give birth without a vet's help.

5. The study revealed a high _____ of birth defects in children whose parents smoked.

## B. Comprehension Check

*Answer the questions.*

1. What do all types of overfishing have in common?

   They can cause _____.

2. What has been the result of overfishing in Africa?

   Reports of illnesses _____.

3. Why did fishing fleets in Newfoundland, Canada, come back empty-handed in 1992?

   The fish population in the area _____.

4. According to the writer, how can we help to eliminate overfishing?

   We should refrain from _____.

## C. Discussion

*Share your opinion with the class.*

Before the discovery of petroleum, whale blubber was the main source of oil. Thus, during the 18th and 19th centuries, the practice of hunting whales was popular, wiping out many species and endangering others. Today, there are still crews who hunt whales. What is your opinion of this issue? How do you think it affects sea life?

# WRITING

## The Classification Essay

Writers break down information into categories to explain a topic.

**In this type of essay:**

☑ Information about the topic is classified by following one guideline.
☑ Each paragraph explains one category and lists examples.
☑ The thesis statement follows this formula:

      [guideline]    [topic]              [categories]

## Task 1

Circle the topic and cross out the subcategory that does not belong.

| 1. | wind | solar | renewable energy | tidal | chemical |
|---|---|---|---|---|---|
| 2. | Siberian tiger | giant panda | blue whale | crocodile | endangered species |
| 3. | household dust | pollutants | hazardous waste | oil spills | factory emissions |

### Parallel Sentence Structure

When listing ideas, use the same word pattern to place equal emphasis on each item.

| **Correct:** | Recycling can take many forms: burying food scraps, finding new uses for old items, and reducing resource consumption. |
|---|---|
| **Incorrect:** | Recycling can take many forms: burying food scraps, new uses for old items, and resource consumption reduction. |

## Task 2

Improve the following topic sentences by fixing the parts in bold.

1. Many people waste water without realizing it by letting water run needlessly, flushing the toilet too often, and **leaky faucets**.
   _____

2. Soil erosion has several causes: strong winds, **raining hard**, and a lack of vegetation.
   _____

3. Environmental science degrees feature **biology class; they also require chemistry and geology**.
   _____

# EXTRA WRITING PRACTICE

## BEFORE YOU WRITE
Match each description to the appropriate ecosystem.

### North American Ecosystems

Desert

Wetland

Tundra

a. Pollutants endanger these areas, like the Florida Everglades.

b. This receives less than 10 inches of rainfall per year.

c. Alaska and northern Canada are home to these icy plains.

d. Water is continuously present in these swamps.

e. The ground is permanently frozen.

f. Freezing temperatures shorten the growing season to 60 days.

g. This exists in Mexico and the western United States.

h. Temperatures can vary as much as 77 degrees within a day.

## WRITE IT UP
Write a 150-word essay classifying the above ecosystems. Include at least two participial phrases.

### Nature Life in North America

**Introduction:** The thesis statement should follow the parallel structure.

The land mass of North America stretches from the North Pole to the equator, allowing many types of environments to exist.

**Body:** Remember each category needs its own paragraph.

**Conclusion:** Summarize the information you've presented.

# UNIT 11

# Expressing Yourself

**Get It Started:**
How many languages do you speak? With the rise of the Internet, we can meet people from all over the world. Why not learn a new language and make more friends? After all, language is the glue that holds us together.

# VOCABULARY

## Task 1

*Match the following words with their correct definitions.* 🎧 2-11

1. accomplish _____
2. symptom _____
3. sharpen _____
4. proficient _____
5. acquisition _____
6. fluency _____
7. résumé _____

a. very good at something
b. a document that describes your education and work experience
c. the process of learning something
d. a change in your body or mind that shows that you have a particular illness
e. to succeed in doing something good
f. the quality of being able to use a language naturally
g. to make something sharp

## Task 2

*Look at the excerpt of an interpreter's résumé. Fill in the blanks with the word choices given.*

> interpreter / acquisition / conveying / complicated / bilingual / articulate

**Objective:**

To work in a challenging position as a 1. _____ Spanish and English 2. _____ in the Immigration Department

**Skills & Qualifications:**

★ Proficient in 3._____ information between Spanish and English speakers

★ Able to 4._____ everything from day-to-day needs to 5._____ political views

★ High 6._____ rate of terminology

# LISTENING & SPEAKING

## A. Comprehension Check

*Listen to the conversation and check **T** if the statement is true, **F** if it's false.* 🎧 2-12

1. **T** ☐ **F** ☐ Kathy's professor doesn't believe that she is a very productive student.

2. **T** ☐ **F** ☐ Kathy and Rick agree that switching between languages in a conversation decreases one's concentration abilities.

3. **T** ☐ **F** ☐ Bilingual people have a lower chance of developing mental diseases.

4. **T** ☐ **F** ☐ Rick plans to gain fluency in another language.

5. **T** ☐ **F** ☐ Kathy thinks that studying languages is a pleasant and effortless experience.

110

## B. Partial Dictation

Listen again and fill in the blanks.  2-12

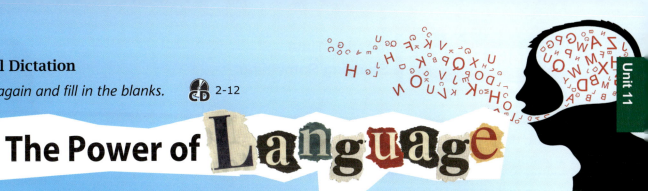

# The Power of Language

*Kathy gets home from school and talks to her brother Rick.*

**Rick:** Hey, Kathy. How was your day?

**Kathy:** Productive. I completed my composition on *Frankenstein* and polished up my résumé.

**Rick:** Wow. You 1. _____ so much while I was just burning daylight.

**burn daylight:** to waste time

**Kathy:** Earlier, my professor asked me how I was able to be so efficient. I said it was because I spoke two languages.

**Rick:** Huh?

**Kathy:** Bilingual 2. _____ has massive benefits for your brain.

**Rick:** Like what?

**Kathy:** Switching between two languages 3. _____ the mind's capability to focus.

**Rick:** That makes sense. When you're speaking one language, you have to inhibit the other to concentrate.

**Kathy:** Exactly. Plus, learning a second language will pay dividends later on. Research suggests that it helps 4. _____ mental diseases that appear during old age, like Alzheimer's.

**pay dividends:** to produce great profits

**Rick:** I've heard about that. Researchers compared patients that had been diagnosed with Alzheimer's and determined that bilingual people maintain higher levels of brain activity.

**Kathy:** Yup. Psychologist Ellen Bialystok also said that their 5. _____ show up four to five years later than average.

**Rick:** I should work on my second language 6. _____.

**Kathy:** It can be pretty tedious.

**Rick:** I'll get the hang of it. How hard can it be?

**get the hang of:** to gradually learn how to do something

**Kathy:** When you're a kid, becoming 7. _____ in a language is your brain's top priority. But now, you have work, school, bills—significant distractions. Adults can't devote as much time to plugging away at a new language.

**plug away:** work hard

**Rick:** Try to keep me accountable by asking how it's going. I 8. _____ give up!

**accountable:** responsible

*Practice the conversation with your partner.*

111

## LANGUAGE FOCUS: Wasting Time / Studying Something

**Wasting Time**

- burn daylight
- fool/hang/mess around
- idle (*time*) away
- goof off

### Task 1

*Work with a classmate and discuss how you waste time with the expressions above. Use the dialog model to help you.*

> **A:** I feel like I'm always burning daylight. When I intend to _____, I fool around _____ instead.
> **B:** I'm not any better. I goof off _____ when I should be _____.
> **A:** Maybe we can hold each other accountable to avoid _____.
> **B:** Good idea!

**Studying Something**

| Learning | • get the hang of (*something*)<br>• get (*something*) down pat<br>• catch on to (*something*) |
|---|---|
| Reviewing | • bone up on (*something*)<br>• brush up on (*something*) |

### Task 2

*Fill in the appropriate expressions. There may be more than one possible answer.*

1. I haven't figured out the technique of ice-skating yet, but I plan to _____.
2. I can't go out tonight. I need to _____ medieval history for my exam tomorrow.
3. Meg is usually great at science, so she'll _____ the concepts.

### Task 3

*Match the two parts.*

1. I know I agreed to brush up on biology with you tonight; _____.
2. Even though I said I would perform at the talent show, _____.
3. I was so distracted that I ended up burning daylight, _____.
4. Despite the fact that I promised to edit your essay for you, _____.
5. Unless you finally get the hang of this math concept, _____.

a. I've just learned that I have to cook dinner for my family
b. I've gotten cold feet and can't go through with it
c. but I'm throwing in the towel because I'm not really improving
d. you won't be able to proceed to the next class
e. so I got nothing accomplished

# GRAMMAR | Indirect Speech

Unit 11

## Types

| Statements | usually introduced by verbs like *say, tell, admit,* and *suggest* | • Research **suggests** that bilingual fluency helps prevent mental diseases that appear during old age. |
|---|---|---|
| Questions | wh- questions | • My professor **asked** me **how** I was able to be so efficient. |
| | yes/no questions | • She **wondered if/whether** I had completed my assignment. |
| Requests/ Commands | affirmative | • The conductor **signaled** the band members **to march**. |
| | negative | • Mom **warned** us **not to chat** with strangers. |

## Tense Changes

The verb tenses are usually changed in indirect speech.

| Simple Present | ⇒ | Simple Past |
|---|---|---|
| Jeff: "My headaches **result** from insufficient sleep." | | Jeff **said** (that) his headaches **resulted** from insufficient sleep. |
| **Present Continuous** | ⇒ | **Past Continuous** |
| Tanya: "I **am preparing** the agenda for the meeting." | | Tanya **explained** that she **was preparing** the agenda for the meeting. |
| **Simple Past / Present Perfect / Past Perfect** | ⇒ | **Past Perfect** |
| Phillip: "I **have** already **modified** the report." | | Phillip **stated** (that) he **had** already **modified** the report. |
| **Present Modal** | ⇒ | **Past Modal** |
| Mr. Anderson: "I **will arrive** before dusk." | | Mr. Anderson **told** me (that) he **would arrive** before dusk. |

## Task

*Change the quotations into indirect speech.*

ex. "Yes, I have eaten there without paying the bill."

Thomas confessed _that he had eaten there without paying the bill_ .

1. "Where did the suspect go after the crime occurred?"
   The police inquired about _____.

2. "You must see a doctor about your throat infection."
   Sean convinced his girlfriend _____.

3. "Are you telling the truth, Mr. Smith?"
   The lawyer asked Mr. Smith _____.

4. "You will be given a total knee replacement."
   The surgeon informed me that _____.

113

# READING

### BEFORE YOU READ  2-13

*Scan the article and write the letter of the communication method used by each animal.*

a. We perform a series of movements to indicate the location of a food source.
b. We change our appearance based on how we feel.
c. We imitate a variety of sounds, including those not made by animals.
d. We move in threatening ways to defend our territory.

 chameleon
 mockingbird
 honeybee
 shark

## What Did It Say?

1   Many pet owners are quick to say that they can communicate with their beloved animals despite not knowing the same language. Animals aren't necessarily able to speak in the same way humans can, but they are undoubtedly capable of communicating, not just between themselves but with
5   people as well.

Dolphins are known for creating countless sounds, ranging from whistles to clicks. Although people can't hear the subtle differences, every sound a dolphin makes is quite distinct. Scientists report that dolphins'
10   language may be just as complex as ours. Of course, they aren't the only animals to communicate with sounds. The majestic melodies that

114

15 birds produce can warn others of predators and attract mates. Each species of bird has its own set of calls, but what's really astonishing is that some birds can become multilingual. They can understand and mimic the calls of other types of birds. Mockingbirds' mastery of this skill is so great that they can learn the sounds of other animals, musical instruments, and even machinery!

20 Other creatures communicate with their bodies and movements. For example, honeybees have one of the most distinctive ways of giving directions—dancing. By using different dance moves, they can let their hive mates know about their discovery of flowers 25 or help lost bees navigate their way back home. Sharks, however, communicate through aggressive gestures. If one shark slams into another, it means that the attacker's territory is being breached. Color is also important in animal communications, and chameleons use it to their advantage. They change their color to indicate their mood, like when they feel threatened or when they 30 are being protective of their space.

When dog owners talk to their pets, they may not realize how much of what they're saying is being understood. An acclaimed American psychologist has applied his expertise on the human brain to the study of our canine companions in order to prove their intelligence. He suggests that the average dog can 35 comprehend around 160 words, which is about the same as a toddler. Some of the most intelligent dog breeds can learn up to 250 words! That's a pretty impressive vocabulary for man's best friend.

With the amount of analysis being done on animal 40 communications, it's obvious that talking to animals isn't a fantasy that only children want to turn into reality!

# AFTER YOU READ

## A. Vocabulary

*Fill in the blanks with the word choices given. Change the word form if necessary.*

> slam / navigate / mastery / companion / astonishing

1. Mark and Jeremy are good traveling _____, as they have compatible personalities and interests.

2. Henry _____ his head on the table when he fell. It hurt so much that he had to go to the hospital.

3. The company has earned _____ profits in the past year. As a result, its stock price continues to soar.

4. Without a map, we'll never be able to _____ our way through this city.

5. His _____ of chess was incredible. He was able to defeat competitors that were much older.

## B. Comprehension Check

*Answer the questions.*

1. According to the article, how do birds communicate?

   Each species of bird has _____
   _____.

2. What do honeybees do to communicate with each other?

   They create _____
   _____.

3. How do sharks react when they feel threatened?

   They make _____
   _____.

4. Why was an American psychologist studying dogs?

   He wanted to prove their cleverness and know _____
   _____.

## C. Discussion

*Share your opinion with the class.*

> It's believed that cats only make sounds to communicate with humans. When they are approached by other animals, they use non-verbal forms of communication. Why do cats interact with humans differently? Can anything be inferred about their intelligence based on this?

# WRITING

### Choose the Best Voice
Once you've identified your audience, choose which voice is most appropriate to use in your writing.

| | |
|---|---|
| first person | narrate personal experiences or opinions |
| second person | instruct or address readers, like in a process analysis essay |
| third person | write about academic topics |

## Task
Answer the questions about the advertisement below.

### Learning a Language in a Flash!

Wish you could converse with people from other cultures? Attempted to learn a second language before but it just didn't stick? Then enroll in The Language Institute, helping people fulfill their language goals since 1975!

In our program, you'll receive one-on-one tutoring to obtain the fastest possible results. Instructors have flexible schedules, so you can study when and where is most convenient for you. Our curriculum is guaranteed to have you chatting away in no time. In fact, if you don't achieve fluency within six months, we'll refund your tuition. So call us today—you've got nothing to lose!

1. Which kind of readers is the author trying to target?
   _____
   _____

2. What do readers likely already know about The Language Institute?
   _____
   _____

3. What kind of language is the writer using to communicate the main point?
   _____
   _____

# EXTRA WRITING PRACTICE

## BEFORE YOU WRITE

*Decide which type of writing the following language facts would be found in. Mark **C** for casual,*
*__I__ for informational, or **A** for academic.*

_____ **a** I think it's crazy that language loss can be caused by businesses, but professionals tend to speak more widely used languages.

_____ **b** Did you know that, according to experts, 50 percent of the world's 6,000 languages are in danger of extinction?

_____ **c** You might find it interesting that each endangered language embodies cultural knowledge of the region in which it is spoken.

_____ **d** These 3,000 endangered languages constitute a largely unknown field that linguists explore.

_____ **e** It's too bad that kids just aren't being taught languages that are only spoken by a few people.

_____ **f** Linguists document languages at risk by recording speech, noting the grammar, and storing the information.

## WRITE IT UP

*Write a 100-word passage about endangered languages for each of the scenarios described below.*
*The first one has already been done for you.*

**Scenario 1:** Alex missed class today, so his classmate is catching him up via e-mail.

You missed an interesting class today! Professor Guinn talked about endangered languages and said that 50 percent of the world's 6,000 languages are about to be lost! I guess that, since business professionals usually speak more widely known languages, parents aren't bothering to teach their kids anything else. So languages slowly die out. Every language has information about the region where it's spoken. Because of this, experts record these languages to study later. Hopefully, this means history will always have them!

**Scenario 2:** Miranda's advisor is sending her information about studying linguistics.

**Scenario 3:** Leo is writing a report for Professor Guinn.

# UNIT 12

# Trends and Fads

## Get It Started:
Do you have the newest smartphone? Is your wardrobe up to date? Keeping up with the latest technology and fashion can be difficult. How important are current trends and fads to you?

# VOCABULARY

## Task 1

Match the following words with their correct definitions.  2-14

1. fad _____
2. visualize _____
3. run-of-the-mill _____
4. inspire _____
5. rewarding _____
6. freak _____
7. duplicate _____

a. to give someone an idea for a book, play, painting, etc.
b. someone who is very interested in something
c. ordinary
d. a style, activity, or interest that is very popular for a short period of time
e. to imagine
f. to make an exact copy of something
g. (of an activity, etc.) worth doing

## Task 2

Fill in the blanks with the word choices given.

sensation / fad / vogue / conventional / staple

### WHAT'S IN RIGHT NOW!

| | |
|---|---|
| Technology | PDAs were a passing 1. _____, and smartphones have since taken over the world. |
| Life | Going green has come into 2. _____ during the past few years. Everyone should take an active role in protecting Mother Earth. |
| Entertainment | Martial arts are a 3. _____ element of Asian entertainment. This film genre appeals to both Eastern and Western audiences. |
| Medicine | More and more people are starting to choose alternative therapies instead of 4. _____ medical practices. |
| Food | Cupcakes are a 5. _____ now. People are crazy about their sweet taste! |

# LISTENING & SPEAKING

### A. Comprehension Check

Listen to the conversation and circle the answers.  2-15

1. What is the purpose of the party?
   a. Ben is overwhelmed by school and wants to take a break.
   b. Jami is throwing a surprise party for her sister.
   c. It will be Ben's birthday soon, and he wants to have a party.

2. Which statement is true?
   a. Most cosplay costumes are purchased from speciality shops.
   b. Although cosplay is new in America, it is starting to catch on.
   c. Only Japanese characters are suitable forms to be copied by cosplayers.

3. What cosplay trend is Jami excited about?
   a. Men can dress up as female characters, and vice versa.
   b. Cosplayers come from countries all over the world.
   c. The popularity of cosplay is growing.

4. How does Jami first feel about making one's own costume?
   a. She feels inspired to sew her own outfit.
   b. She thinks it sounds time-consuming.
   c. She feels that the idea is old-fashioned.

B. **Partial Dictation**

Listen again and fill in the blanks. 🎧 2-15

# Sensational Cosplay

Ben's birthday is coming up, and Jami wants to celebrate it.

**Jami:** How do you want to celebrate your birthday?

**Ben:** What about a cosplay party?

**Jami:** That seems far out for Americans.

**Ben:** It's becoming all the rage! I had been cosplaying until I had to take a break because of my heavy school load, but now I'm back!

**Jami:** That's because you're an eccentric science fiction 1. _____.

**Ben:** Hey!

**Jami:** I'm just kidding. My friend said that the participants were mainly 2. _____ by their favorite manga and anime characters when this 3. _____ first started. Is that true?

**Ben:** Yes. However, costumes from series like *Star Wars* and *Harry Potter* are also run-of-the-mill nowadays.

**Jami:** I want to get all decked out as Hermione then.

**Ben:** People had only been taking part as characters of their own 4. _____ before, but now it's common to wear costumes of either sex. So you could be a male character if you like.

**Jami:** It's awesome that it's not 5. _____ anymore! Where can I buy a costume?

**Ben:** Cosplayers make their own 6. _____.

**Jami:** Isn't making your own clothes rather out of date?

**Ben:** No way! A major motivation behind cosplay is producing a unique costume. It's a fun way to express your creativity.

**Jami:** I know what you mean. 7. _____ a costume and then bringing your fantasy to life would be rewarding.

**Ben:** Cosplayers often educate themselves in handicrafts like sewing and woodworking in order to 8. _____ a costume more accurately.

**Jami:** Well, I do love crafts!

far out: too strange

all the rage: fashionable

get decked out: to dress up

bring something to life: to make something more exciting

**Practice the conversation with your partner.**

# LANGUAGE FOCUS
Talking About Unusual and Common Things
Discussing Fashions

## Talking About Unusual and Common Things

| Unusual | Common |
|---|---|
| • be far out | • be run-of-the-mill |
| • be something else | • be a dime a dozen |
| • be out in left field | • be nothing out of the ordinary |

## Task 1

*Pair up with a classmate and discuss what you consider unusual and common about the following topics using the expressions above.*

| | | |
|---|---|---|
| cosplay | experiments on animals | online shopping |
| bullying in schools | makeup for men | human cloning |

*Example*

A: Did you hear about that comic book convention downtown?
B: Yeah. Those people who dress up like the characters from the comics **are** really **far out**.

## Discussing Fashions

| Fashionable | Old-fashioned |
|---|---|
| • be all the rage | • be out of date |
| • be in vogue/fashion/style | • go out of vogue/fashion/style |
| • be the latest thing | • be behind the times |

## Task 2

*Improve the parts in bold using the expressions above. There may be more than one possible answer.*

A: Did you see Karen's dress last night? **It was stunning!**

⇒ _____.

B: I know. **She always wears sensational clothes.**

⇒ _____.

A: Definitely. Compared to her, I feel like I look **unfashionable**.

⇒ Compared to her, I feel like I look _____.

B: That's not true! **You wear lots of trendy stuff.**

⇒ _____.

122

# GRAMMAR | Past Perfect Continuous

Unit 12

The past perfect continuous tense is used to talk about events that took place in the past for a long time before other past events occurred.

## Usage

| To show that something was in progress until another time in the past | I had been cosplaying until I had to take a break because of my heavy school load. |
|---|---|
| To talk about causes in the recent past | Mary purchased a new jacket because she had been needing one since the previous winter. |
| To report something said in the past | Liz said her husband had been verbally abusing her for a long time. |
| To form third conditional sentences | If you hadn't been sending text messages on your phone, we wouldn't have gotten into this accident. |

## Tense Comparisons

| Present Perfect Continuous | Past Perfect Continuous |
|---|---|
| Used for events that began in the past and continue in the present | Used for events that began in the past and ended just recently |
| The award-winning director has been making films since the 1960s. (*He's still making films.*) | The award-winning director who had been making films since the 1960s retired this week. (*He made films until recently.*) |

| Past Perfect | Past Perfect Continuous |
|---|---|
| Used for non-continuous events that occurred before another past event | Used for events that lasted for a while before another past event |
| James had failed to gain admission to the university three times before he was accepted. | The girl had been groaning in pain for 30 minutes before she was taken to the hospital. |

| Past Continuous | Past Perfect Continuous |
|---|---|
| Used for events that lasted for a while in the past | Used for past events that lasted for a while and caused something to happen |
| He was practicing for his presentation all night. | The reason he did so well during his presentation was because he had been practicing every night. |

## Task

*Choose the correct tenses.*

The city officials 1.( **are suggesting** / **had been suggesting** ) building a subway line for the previous few months. While some people 2.( **were** / **being** ) opposed to the development of the area because of its archaeological importance, others 3. ( **are agreeing** / **had been agreeing** ) with the idea. Then came the find of the century. One section of the line 4. ( **hidden** / **had been hiding** ) an ancient burial ground. Several large tombs 5.( **lie** / **had been lying** ) underground for ages. The archaeologists 6.( **have urged** / **had been urging** ) the government to cancel the project only days before the discovery, and now it seems that their plan to construct a museum may not have been wishful thinking. Many developers, however, 7.( **have been voicing** / **were voicing** ) complaints that a line built elsewhere would be too costly. An agreement still 8.( **hasn't been** / **isn't** ) reached.

123

# READING

## BEFORE YOU READ  🎧 2-16

*Scan the reading and match the people with the dangerous beauty practices they are known for.*

### People
1. Egyptians: _____
2. Greeks and Romans: _____
3. Queen Elizabeth I: _____
4. Lady Gaga: _____

### Beauty Practice
a. White lead powder on the face
b. Drops of nightshade in the eyes
c. Black lead liner around the eyes
d. Special contact lenses

# Dying to Be Beautiful

1   When one hears about plastic surgery nightmares and eating disorders, it's easy to assume that obsession with beauty is only a modern-day phenomenon. The truth is that numerous beauty practices had been damaging health long before the present time.

The ancient Egyptians were the first to embrace cosmetics as
5   a way of life. When looking at paintings of them, the first thing one will notice is their dark eyeliner. They applied it because they believed it could ward off evil spirits. Unfortunately, the substance they used was made from lead, which not only resulted in eye infections but also mental diseases. Ancient
10   Greeks and Romans took the use of lead even further by grinding it into a white powder and covering their faces with it. Since they used so much more, they suffered harsher consequences, such as insanity and paralysis.

124

Thanks to Queen Elizabeth I, in the 1500s it was routine to enlarge one's pupils with the toxic nightshade plant. It makes the eyes look brighter, but constant use can prove fatal. Furthermore, it wasn't just cosmetics that had been presenting problems. It was during this century that corsets became popular. The tight underwear was worn to shrink the size of the wearer's waist, but it could lead to breathing difficulty and even defects of the spine.

Today, famous people are still used as fashion barometers. Lady Gaga's style is one that is frequently copied. In one of her music videos, the pop star wore special contact lenses that made her eyes look bigger. Impressed by the look, teenagers began purchasing similar contacts. However, while the items hadn't been harming the singer, others have complained of side effects ranging from irritation to blindness. In terms of footwear, high-heeled shoes have long been known to contribute to knee and foot issues, but this hasn't decreased their popularity. The current passion for skinny jeans is also harmful. When the jeans are too tight, they can cause nerve damage and numbness in the legs.

By observing the trends in recent years, it can be hard to imagine a time in the future when people will no longer be suffering in the name of beauty. Will people ever stop this dangerous search for the perfect look?

# AFTER YOU READ

## A. Vocabulary

*Fill in the blanks with the word choices given. Change the word form if necessary.*

> spine / obsession / defect / barometer / consequence

1. Robert's _____ with the local baseball team is so great that he has been to every one of their games this season.

2. One of the _____ of failing a class is that you'll eventually have to retake it.

3. Darren's _____ was damaged in the accident, and it is unlikely that he will ever walk again.

4. The girl was born with a heart _____, so she's been taking medication all her life.

5. The number of newly established businesses is a good _____ of the state of the economy.

## B. Comprehension Check

*Write the paragraph number next to the matching main idea.*

| Paragraph | Main Idea |
|---|---|
| | Modern beauty practices are the source of several medical problems. |
| | The world's first cosmetics were made from substances that caused severe damage. |
| | In this era, people made use of both fatal cosmetics and tight clothing. |
| | It is unlikely that harmful approaches for obtaining perfection will ever die out. |
| | Throughout history, people have taken risks in their quest to look more attractive. |

*Check **T** if the statement is true, **F** if it's false.*

1. T ☐ F ☐ The ancient Egyptians wore makeup to defend themselves against illnesses.

2. T ☐ F ☐ Corsets were a type of clothing that were worn to stretch a person's abdomen.

3. T ☐ F ☐ Unusual contact lenses became more popular with teenagers due to their appearance on Lady Gaga.

4. T ☐ F ☐ In previous generations, high-heeled shoes were not as destructive to one's health.

5. T ☐ F ☐ People who wear skinny jeans have reported some loss of feeling in the legs.

## C. Discussion

*Share your opinion with the class.*

Nowadays, permanent cosmetics are gaining popularity. Tattoos are used to resemble makeup that people normally apply every day, from eyeliner to lipstick. Although the technique is time-saving, it does have numerous risks, such as scars and infections. Do you think the effort is worthwhile? Would you ever consider having the procedure done?

# WRITING

Unit 12

## The Opinion Essay

In an opinion essay, explain your viewpoint on a topic by including:

☑ **Reasons why you feel the way you do**

☑ **Facts, observations, and examples to support your perspective**

Strongly state your opinion without being rude. Which phrases below are appropriate?

| | | |
|---|---|---|
| ☐ I guess | ☐ my personal view is | ☐ it's ridiculous to think |
| ☐ I'm convinced | ☐ I suppose | ☐ in my opinion |
| ☐ I would argue | ☐ a popular belief is | ☐ I firmly believe |

## Task 1

*Rewrite each sentence below to make it more appropriate for an opinion essay. Is there an opinion? Is the language informal?*

1. Yoga supporters say that side effects such as muscle tears and joint damage can be avoided, but that is unlikely.

   → _____

2. Well, if you ask me, pop stars like Justin Bieber and Selena Gomez are way too young to be getting so much attention from the media.

   → _____

## Task 2

*Rewrite the author's opinion in your own words. List the support given.*

In the foreseeable future, making purchases will no longer necessitate paper money. The use of cash has been diminishing since the advent of credit cards. Now, Google and MasterCard are collaborating to create a computerized payment system that uses mobile phones. Obviously, paying with these everyday items is infinitely more convenient because they are easier to tuck into a pocket or purse. Not to mention, most people already habitually carry their cell phones. Plus, users can easily cancel a stolen card or misplaced phone to protect their financial accounts. And, as trees are necessary to print the paper for bills, these systems have the additional benefit of being ecofriendly. Hopefully, companies will be able to implement these measures soon.

**Writer's Opinion** _____

_____

**Supporting Detail** _____

_____

_____

127

## EXTRA WRITING PRACTICE

### BEFORE YOU WRITE

*Interview three classmates about the topics below. Note their opinions in addition to your own. Remember to include support.*

**Fast Facts** **Organic Cosmetics**

- The Environmental Working Group (EWG) discovered that 28 percent of non-organic lipstick products contained substances associated with cancer risk.
- The President's Cancer Panel revealed that only 11 percent of regular beauty products' ingredients have been tested for safety.

Are cosmetics damaging to your skin?

**Fast Facts** **Angry Birds**

- Over 12 million copies of the game have been bought, making it one of the most purchased apps.
- When playing the game, gamers reported feeling addicted:

| Never | 18% | Occasionally | 54% |
|-------|-----|--------------|-----|
| Often | 15% | Always | 13% |

Should children be allowed to play Angry Birds?

### WRITE IT UP

*Write a 150-word opinion essay about one of the above topics. Use the past perfect continuous if possible.*

**Title:** _____ (Be creative.)

**Introduction:**
Include opinion words in your thesis statement.

**Body:**
Support your perspective with facts and examples. Use strong language to communicate your opinion.

**Conclusion:**
Restate your position.

# UNIT 13

# Seeing the World

### Get It Started:
Did you know that it is illegal not to flush a public toilet in Singapore? It seems unbelievable, but it's true! Every country has its own laws and culture. Let's take a look at different types of tourism and what to keep in mind when traveling.

# VOCABULARY

## Task 1
Match the following words with their correct definitions.  2-17

1. regulation ____
2. expedition ____
3. stereotype ____
4. breach ____
5. deport ____
6. fine ____
7. substantial ____

a. large in amount
b. to force someone to leave a country
c. an official rule or order
d. a set idea that people have about what someone or something is like
e. to break a law, rule, or agreement
f. money that you have to pay as a punishment
g. an organized journey with a particular purpose

## Task 2
Fill in the blanks with the word choices given.

| funds / conscious / endangered / excursions / worsen / popularity |
| --- |

### Last Chance Tourism

Society is becoming more environmentally 1._____.
This trend has contributed to the 2._____ of Last Chance Tourism, which features travel to threatened regions, such as the Maldives. This practice both increases awareness of environmental issues and raises 3._____ to restore the areas. The 4._____, however, also have negative effects, and environmentalists question whether tourism is actually further damaging these 5._____ places. After all, the multitudes of visitors only 6._____ the problems.

# LISTENING & SPEAKING

### A. Comprehension Check

Listen to the conversation and check **T** if the statement is true, **F** if it's false. 2-18

1. T ☐ F ☐ Valerie believes that Tyler would benefit from her advice about proper behavior in other countries.
2. T ☐ F ☐ Although chewing gum has been forbidden in Singapore, Tyler doesn't care about being caught doing it.
3. T ☐ F ☐ According to Valerie, it is unacceptable to flush the toilet in Switzerland before sunset.
4. T ☐ F ☐ If you feed some of the birds in Venice, you will need to pay a fine.
5. T ☐ F ☐ The most substantial penalty Valerie mentions is the one that is given to those who litter in Malaysia.

**B. Partial Dictation**

Listen again and fill in the blanks.  2-18

# When in Rome, Do as the Romans Do

Tyler and Valerie are discussing an approaching trip.

**Tyler:** I'm thrilled about the worldwide 1. _____ we're going to take.

**Valerie:** Me too, but you should be concerned about the strict laws in the countries we'll be traveling to.

**Tyler:** Really? I thought they all had similar 2. _____.

**Valerie:** You're way off! Some routine things we do are illegal or taboo overseas.

**way off:** completely wrong

**Tyler:** What do you mean?

**Valerie:** It's imperative to become acquainted with the basic laws of 3. _____ country you plan to visit. Otherwise, you could unintentionally break laws however hard you try not to.

**imperative:** very important

**Tyler:** Tell me more. I don't want to fit the stereotype of the ignorant tourist.

**ignorant:** not knowing enough about something

**Valerie:** Take Singapore, for example. It outlawed 4. _____ gum in 1992, and enforcement is rigid.

**Tyler:** OK. Then I'll just chew some when we take our cruise to Malaysia.

**Valerie:** Fine. And while we're in Switzerland, remember that 5. _____ you flush the toilet, be sure to check the time. We'll land in hot water if we flush after 10:00 p.m.

**land in hot water:** to get into trouble

**Tyler:** Flushing is against the law?

**Valerie:** Many local residents refrain from flushing so as not to disturb their neighbors. In Singapore, however, not flushing a public toilet incurs a 6. _____ fine.

**Tyler:** So always flush in Singapore, but look at the time first in Switzerland.

**Valerie:** That's right on the money. Our final stop is Venice, where the government has cracked down on 7. _____ pigeons. You can be fined €500 for such an offense.

**right on the money:** correct

**crack down on:** to become more strict in dealing with a problem

**€:** = Euro

**Tyler:** You've got to be kidding! Hopefully, I won't get deported if I end up 8. _____ any of these laws!

*Practice the conversation with your partner.*

131

# LANGUAGE FOCUS

Discussing Being Right and Wrong
Getting into Difficult Situations

## Discussing Being Right and Wrong

| Accurate | Inaccurate |
|---|---|
| • be (right) on the money<br>• be spot on<br>• hit the nail on the head | • be way off<br>• be off base<br>• be off the mark |

### Task 1

*Pair up with a classmate. Discuss if you think the quotes below are right or wrong by using the expressions above.*

An insincere and evil friend is more to be feared than a wild beast; a wild beast may wound your body, but an evil friend will wound your mind.—*Buddha*

There are no regrets in life, just lessons.—*Jennifer Aniston*

Be thankful for what you have; you'll end up having more. If you concentrate on what you don't have, you will never, ever have enough.—*Oprah Winfrey*

## Getting into Difficult Situations

- be in trouble
- be up the creek (without a paddle)
- get in a bind
- be in a tight spot
- be in hot water

### Task 2

*Discuss the following situations with a partner using the expressions.*

1. You max out your credit card.
2. You miss your flight for New Year.
3. You tip over while riding in a canoe.

# GRAMMAR | Wh-ever Words

Unit 13

## Wh-ever and No Matter

Wh-ever words and no matter who, what, which, where, when, and how can be used to join clauses. The meaning is similar to the following: it is not important who/what/which/where/when/how.

| No Matter | Wh-ever |
|---|---|
| • **No matter where** you want to go, the satellite navigation system will direct you there.<br>• **No matter when** you need assistance, do not hesitate to contact us. | • **Wherever** you want to go, the satellite navigation system will direct you there.<br>• **Whenever** you need assistance, do not hesitate to contact us. |

### Usage Note

Clauses that begin with wh-ever words can be used as subjects or objects. Clauses that begin with no matter cannot be.

*ex.* **Whatever** the controversial artist does will cause quite a stir.
(No matter what the controversial artist does will cause quite a stir.)

It's imperative to become acquainted with the basic laws of **whichever** country you plan to visit.
(It's imperative to become acquainted with the basic laws of no matter which country you plan to visit.)

## Function

| adverbs | You could unintentionally break laws **however** hard you try not to. |
|---|---|
| conjunctions | While we're in Switzerland, remember that **whenever** you flush the toilet, be sure to check the time. |
| determiners (whichever, whatever) | Make sure you return **whichever** DVD you decide to borrow from me tomorrow. |
| in noun clauses | **Whatever** was said in the news report was absolutely baseless and inappropriate. |
| in relative clauses | The three representatives, **whomever** the community elects, will attend the press conference on Wednesday. |
| in informal responses | A: Do you want to go out to eat or make dinner at home?<br>B: **Whatever**. (*Whatever you want to do.*) |

## Task

*Match the two parts.*

1. I would like to make an appointment to see the physician _____.

2. In my opinion, whichever freeway you take during rush hour _____.

3. The assistant was instructed to hold all calls _____.

4. Whoever receives the highest score on the oral examination _____.

5. The anniversary celebration is open _____.

a. for whoever had meetings during the afternoon

b. to however many people want to attend

c. is entitled to skip the next pop quiz

d. is sure to be a traffic nightmare

e. whenever there is an open slot available

133

# READING

**BEFORE YOU READ**  2-19

*Take a look at the introduction of the article and choose which type of traveler would be most interested in reading it.*

a. A business executive who is looking to take a relaxing two-week excursion
b. An elderly person who dreams of traveling the world during retirement
c. A backpacker who is short on cash but wants to experience exotic cultures
d. A busy parent who is a travel enthusiast but needs to choose a place that caters to kids

# Get Rich Quick by Traveling!

1  Working abroad can be an amazing experience, and opportunities for getting a working holiday visa are a dime a dozen. For many adventure seekers, however, typical jobs are too commonplace. If this describes you, rest assured that there are other unique ways to earn
5  money while traveling.

For those interested in agricultural practices and working on their tans, farming is ideal. Wherever you're headed, it's likely that World Wide Opportunities on Organic Farms (WWOOF) has a job opening at your destination. Workers can harvest orchards in the
10  US, herd sheep in Iceland, or tend to horses in Australia. In addition to a salary, most estates offer communal lodging and meals. Whichever job you choose, you will have the chance to soak up a new culture and meet a diverse group of people. The only requirement is the capability to work hard.

134

15    By working as an au pair, young adults can explore an unfamiliar society while building close relationships. There are many international agencies that connect travelers with families willing to host them. In exchange for an allowance, accommodation, and language classes, the au pair assists
20    with daily domestic chores. Responsibilities can include cooking, vacuuming, and babysitting. But an au pair isn't just a servant or nanny. This French term literally means "living on equal terms," and whoever winds up hosting you should anticipate embracing you as a relative. Elin
25    Nordegren was actually introduced to her former husband, Tiger Woods, by the family she was working for as an au pair!

    Instead of spending money on traveling overseas, make some while working as part of a ship's crew. While naval experience is preferable, it is not necessarily required. Culinary, mechanical, or navigational skills could also make you a valuable candidate for a position
30    on deck. If you'd like to work on a more luxurious vessel, try a cruise ship. A sure way to get hired is by having expertise in something that could entertain passengers, like dealing cards in a casino, coordinating children's activities, or dancing professionally. The best approach for finding an open post is to show up at a pier ready to go.

35    If you've grown weary of run-of-the-mill tourist attractions, maybe it's time to visit foreign countries differently. Not only can working while overseas put more money in your pocket, but it will also help you see the world with new eyes.

# AFTER YOU READ

## A. Vocabulary

*Fill in the blanks with the word choices given. Change the word form if necessary.*

> anticipate / weary / diverse / coordinate / assured

1. You can rest _____ that the dress will be completed in time for your wedding.

2. The shop stocked a _____ range of items for tourists—souvenirs and local snacks.

3. The scientist _____ objections to his theory, so he prepared evidence to prove it.

4. I was asked to _____ the event, but I just don't have enough time to do it.

5. I've been going out wih the same people to the same places for many years and I've grown _____ of it.

## B. Comprehension Check

*Answer the questions.*

1. Besides a paycheck, what does the author think are the benefits of working overseas on a farm?

   The benefits include _____.

2. How is an au pair different from a servant or nanny?

   They are treated like _____.

3. If you want to save money on transportation costs, what could you do?

   You could _____.

4. What experiences would give you an advantage when applying for a position on board a sailing vessel?

   Knowing how to _____
   _____ could make you a preferable candidate.

## C. Discussion

*Share your opinion with the class.*

A staggering 76 percent of young adults who studied or worked abroad for at least two months reported acquiring skills that swayed their career choices. Of the same group, 62 percent asserted that the experience ignited interest in a new vocation. Why do you think this is? If you were to work in a foreign country, what position would you pursue?

# WRITING

## The Narrative Essay

In a narrative essay, a writer includes three essential elements.

- ✓ **Character.** Use concrete details to make your characters more realistic.
- ✓ **Setting.** Provide readers with details like the place and time.
- ✓ **Plot.** Arrange events in order of introduction, rising action, climax, and resolution.

### Task 1

Check the sentences that include concrete narrative details.

1. Texas turned out to be kind of a rotten place to take my vacation.
2. Alexis wildly kicked at her attacker, desperate to escape from him.
3. Mason stood in awe of the prehistoric temple, staring up at its crumbling marble.
4. The horse looked terrifying, so I felt really nervous about riding it.
5. The evening air felt refreshingly cool as they watched the glittering sunset.

### Task 2

Using your imagination, improve the passage by including concrete details.

I flew off to Hong Kong for a week with my best friend, Kimmie. On our first day, we caught a bus to get from our hostel to Victoria Harbor. We got lost. Luckily, we happened to find the bus as we were wandering around.

# EXTRA WRITING PRACTICE

## BEFORE YOU WRITE
*Answer the questions using the suggestions to give you ideas. Be as descriptive as possible.*

### A Nightmare Trip

- Where did you go, when did you travel there, and who went with you?
- What bad things happened?
  > Food poisoning made me vomit like crazy.
- Was the entire trip bad or were there enjoyable parts, too?
  > My passport was stolen, and I had to wait for my replacement to arrive, so I was able to enjoy a few more days of vacation!

### My Dream Vacation

- Whom do you want to travel with?
- Where do you want to go and why?
  > I dream of going to Prague to tour its Baroque style castles and cathedrals.
- During which season would you go?
  > Prague is spectacular in the autumn because of the colors of the trees.

## WRITE IT UP
Write a 160-word narrative essay describing one of the scenarios above. Use the vocabulary from the unit and include wh-ever words if possible.

**Title:** _____ (Be creative.)

**Introduction:** Introduce the setting of the story.

**Body:** Don't forget the rising action and climax.

**Conclusion:** Wrap up all the details and write your resolution.

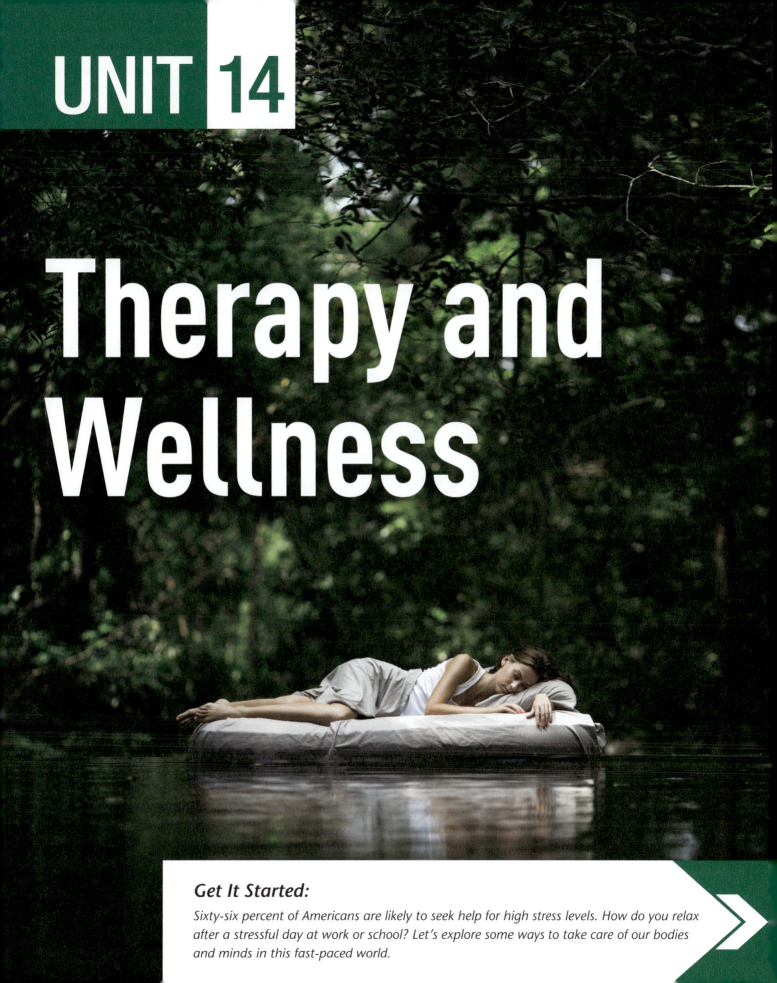

# UNIT 14
# Therapy and Wellness

**Get It Started:**
*Sixty-six percent of Americans are likely to seek help for high stress levels. How do you relax after a stressful day at work or school? Let's explore some ways to take care of our bodies and minds in this fast-paced world.*

## VOCABULARY

### Task 1
Match the following words with their correct definitions.  2-20

1. clinical      _____    a. a sudden rapid increase in how often something bad happens
2. instinctive   _____    b. to affect someone in an unpleasant way
3. afflict       _____    c. following one after another in a series
4. addicted      _____    d. not able to stop doing something as a habit
5. humiliating   _____    e. embarrassing
6. epidemic      _____    f. relating to treating people who are sick
7. consecutive   _____    g. reacting naturally and without thinking

### Task 2
Fill in the blanks with the correct forms of the word choices given. There may be more than one possible answer.

> induce / soothe / combat / supplement / alleviate / relieve

**Health Facts**

1. For some people, even the intake of a small amount of nuts can _____ a serious allergic reaction.
2. According to the brochure, these herbs can be used to _____ pain and swelling in the joints.
3. In order to _____ aggressive forms of cancer, surgery may be required.
4. When you are afflicted with any virus, you should _____ your diet with vitamin C.

## LISTENING & SPEAKING

### A. Comprehension Check

Listen to the conversation and circle the answers.   2-21

1. Why does Peter suspect that Sam has Internet addiction disorder?
   a. He spent almost eight hours online in one day.
   b. He stayed up all night playing computer games.
   c. He played video games for 24 consecutive hours.

2. How many Internet users are estimated to suffer from addiction?
   a. Only a few percent
   b. Five percent
   c. Up to 10 percent

3. According to Peter, what are the symptoms of Internet addiction disorder?
   a. Addicts often become violent.
   b. Going online becomes a habit.
   c. Addicts hardly sleep at night.

4. What does Peter believe Sam should do to overcome his problem?
   a. To enter a rehabilitation facility
   b. To bail out on friends and family
   c. To sell his computer

**B. Partial Dictation**

Listen again and fill in the blanks. 2-21

# Internet Abuse and Addiction

*Peter walks into his dorm room and notices Sam using the computer.*

**Peter:** Hey, Sam. How long have you been on the computer?

**Sam:** Since around 9:00 this morning.

**Peter:** It's almost 5:00! You will have been surfing the Internet for eight hours in just a few minutes!

**Sam:** How did I lose track of the time?

**Peter:** Maybe you're 1. _____ to the Internet.

**Sam:** Oh, please.

**Peter:** Wake up and smell the coffee, Sam! Internet addiction disorder is a clinical condition. It's becoming an epidemic, 2. _____ up to 10 percent of web users.

**Sam:** Geez. What are the symptoms?

**Peter:** Getting online becomes 3. _____; you don't care about having physical interactions with others. In the worst-case scenario, addicts totally bail out on friends and family.

**Sam:** Come on. You're depicting things way too 4. _____.

**Peter:** Stop burying your head in the sand. Go find a rehabilitation center and get help.

**Sam:** But what if others found out? That would be 5. _____.

**Peter:** Well, by the time you do admit you need help, your condition will have been 6. _____ for so long that you might be beyond 7. _____.

**Sam:** OK. I guess you're right. Do you know what the facilities are like?

**Peter:** Therapists combat the addiction by using group sessions, art therapy, and brain stimulation.

**Sam:** Perhaps it is time to bite the bullet. I don't want to be like that guy who played video games for 780 consecutive hours—even *I* think that's 8. _____.

**Peter:** It'll be tough, but I'll stand by you all the way.

**Practice the conversation with your partner.**

---

**lose track:** to fail to know what is happening to someone

**wake up and smell the coffee:** to pay attention to what's going on

**bail out:** to stop being involved with something

**bury one's head in the sand:** to ignore an unpleasant situation

**bite the bullet:** to start to deal with an unpleasant situation

# LANGUAGE FOCUS

Being Supportive and Unsupportive
Facing the Consequences

## Being Supportive and Unsupportive

| Supporting | Abandoning |
| --- | --- |
| • stand by (*someone*) | • bail out on (*someone*) |
| • stick by/with (*someone*) | • leave (*someone*) high and dry |
| • back (*someone*) up | • turn (*one's*) back on (*someone*) |

### Task 1

*Pair up with a classmate and discuss situations when you were supported or abandoned by the following people. Use the expressions above.*

| parents | best friend |
| --- | --- |
| roommate or neighbor | brother or sister |
| classmate or colleague | teacher or superior |

*Example*

- My sister and I always **stand by** each other. She took care of me during my entire hospital stay for my surgery. I really appreciate that she didn't **leave** me **high and dry**.

## Facing the Consequences

- bite the bullet
- face the music
- pay the piper
- take (*one's*) medicine

### Task 2

*Rewrite the parts in bold using the expressions above. Then act out the situation with a classmate.*

A: I can't believe you scratched Mr. Randolf's scooter! I guess you'll have to **go tell him**.

⇒ _____.

B: It was an accident. Plus, you wrecked his garden when you were skating last night. You'll also need to **explain what you did**.

⇒ _____.

A: Do you think he'll tell our parents about this?

B: Probably. And then we'll have to **accept our punishment** from them, too.

⇒ _____.

## GRAMMAR | Future Perfect Continuous

Unit 14

The future perfect continuous tense is used to talk about future actions that will be in progress when another event occurs.

### Types

| will have been + present participle | You **will have been surfing** the Internet for eight hours in just a few minutes! |
| --- | --- |
| am/is/are + going to have been + present participle | I **am going to have been renting** this apartment for six months come July 15. |

### Usage

| To show that something continues until a certain time in the future | By the time you do admit you need help, your condition **will have been worsening** for so long that you might be beyond cure. |
| --- | --- |
| To express the cause of a future happening | Gloria will be an expert in geology when she begins teaching because she **is going to have been working** in the field for a whole decade. |

### Special Rules

| 1. The future perfect continuous stops at or before sometime in the future. The verb in the time clause takes the simple present. |
| --- |
| When Jim turns [~~will turn~~] 65, he **will have been working** at the university for more than 40 years. |
| 2. Use the present perfect continuous in clauses starting with time expressions. |
| You won't become an accomplished guitarist until you **have been playing** [~~will have been playing~~] for several years. |
| 3. When we do not include time words or phrases, we often use the future continuous. |
| Chris will be relaxed because he **will be cruising** in the Caribbean. |
| 4. The future perfect continuous emphasizes a length of time during which something will happen. Use the future perfect to emphasize an amount of something. |
| Maggie **will have been cooking** for three hours once you finally show up to help her. *(emphasizes a length of time)* <br> Maggie **will have finished** baking three pies before we get to her house tonight. *(emphasizes the number of pies)* |

### Task

*Match the two parts.*

1. I think the contractors are going to have been _____.

2. When you see the intersection of High Street and Main Street, _____.

3. On Tuesday, the search to find survivors of the earthquake _____.

4. When I finish this year's marathon, _____.

5. After he completes his certification course, _____.

a. you will have been driving for at least 30 minutes

b. will have been continuing for two weeks

c. working on this construction site for over a year before they finish laying the foundation

d. he is going to have been practicing medicine for three years

e. I will have been running for six years

143

# READING

## BEFORE YOU READ 🎧 2-22

Take a look at the title, first paragraph, and subtitles. What do you think the reading will be about?

a. The procedures that one should follow in order to become an alternative medicine practitioner
b. Unconventional therapies that are being used to relieve common medical complaints
c. The steps that a treatment must go through before it is considered mainstream
d. Illnesses that most people suffer from and how they are effectively treated

# The Changing Face of Alternative Medicine

1   Every day, alternative medicine is utilized by practitioners to aid their patients. Some forms, like acupuncture*, are so widespread that they no longer seem unusual. Others appear bizarre, and it might be a long time before they go mainstream. However, the next time you suffer from an
5   illness, you might be surprised by the profound results these therapies can achieve. Your perception of their healing properties could quickly change.

### Doctor Fish

If you want to give your feet a more youthful look, make an appointment with the doctor fish. From
10   Turkey to Japan, these tiny physicians have become part of a spa treatment that entails them feeding on your feet. There's no need to worry though because they only eat dead skin cells. Those who give this treatment a try swear their feet emerge from the
15   water fresh, healthy, and soft.

### Beer Spa

The Chodovar Brewery* is an establishment in the Czech Republic that has earned a reputation for producing the region's best beers. Besides tasting good, the beverage is said to have amazing effects on the body. Large tubs have been installed in the brewery's cellars so that guests can soak in gallons of heated beer. A 20-minute session reportedly relieves a person's acne, soothes painful joints, and improves circulation. Since bathers can also enjoy a pint or two of the beer during the relaxation period, they are required to rest after getting out.

### Cryotherapy

The use of ice to alleviate pain is well-known, so what about putting one's entire body in a place colder than a block of ice? That's what happens at the Olympic Sports Center in Poland.

Wearing only a swimming suit, socks, gloves, and a hat, individuals receiving treatment are placed inside of a chamber cooled to minus 120 degrees Celsius. During the procedure, the patient will only have to stand in the chamber for a few minutes, but the effects will last for weeks. Those that have undergone this process of whole-body cryotherapy claim that it has awesome effects on sore muscles. Many also say it is so energizing that they feel their stress melt away immediately.

By the time future treatments are unveiled, alternative medicine will have been dazzling remedy seekers for many years. There's no telling what innovative cures therapists will come up with next.

[**Notes**] * **acupuncture**: a form of traditional Chinese medicine involving needles
* **brewery**: a factory for making beer

# AFTER YOU READ

## A. Vocabulary

*Fill in the blanks with the word choices given. Change the word form if necessary.*

> establishment / unveil / profound / beverage / circulation

1. The heart is responsible for blood _____ throughout the body.

2. Every _____ on this street had to close for a week as a result of road construction.

3. The friendships made during childhood will have _____ effects on one's character.

4. _____ were offered to everyone who attended the event.

5. When the company _____ the plans to move its headquarters to a different city, the employees were shocked.

## B. Comprehension Check

*Write the therapy (doctor fish, beer spa, or cryotherapy) next to the matching description.*
*There may be more than one possible answer.*

1. Only minimal clothing is worn, despite the freezing temperature.          _____

2. This procedure is appropriate for removing the outer layer of one's skin.          _____

3. One must refrain from movement after completing this form of therapy.          _____

4. Those that have undergone this treatment feel less tense when it is over.          _____

5. To experience this, one must travel underground where the principal ingredient is stored.          _____

6. This is beneficial to both parties since the practitioner receives nourishment from the patient.          _____

## C. Discussion

*Share your opinion with the class.*

> Many Americans had not heard of acupuncture until 1972, when reporter James Reston visited China. During his stay, Reston was treated by a practitioner of Chinese medicine. Intrigued by the process, he wrote an article about it for *The New York Times*. What do you think about the popularity of Chinese medicine in the West? Have you ever had acupuncture before? What is your opinion about its use?

# WRITING

## Paraphrasing vs. Summarizing

- A paraphrase is a restatement of a passage in the writer's own words. Typically, it explains or clarifies the original text.
- A summary is a shorter, simpler version of a passage. It highlights the major points from the original text.

### Attributing Sources

Paraphrased or summarized ideas must be attributed to their origin. Use phrases like *according to*, *as reported by*, and *as stated in*.

## Task 1
*Paraphrase the facts presented below.*

1. *Shiatsu*, which is a Japanese word meaning "finger pressure," is the practice of pounding and stretching the human body to improve vigor.
   → _____
   _____

2. Mongolian *bariachis* are people who manipulate broken bones back into proper position without the use of medicine or instruments.
   → _____
   _____

## Task 2
*Summarize the following passage in two to three sentences.*

It is believed that the Egyptians were the first civilization to discover the medical uses of aloe vera. Known as "the plant of immortality," it was presented as a burial gift to the pharaohs as far back as 6,000 years ago. The clear gel inside the leaves of aloe vera plants is effective for various skin conditions, such as burns, wounds, and sunburns. Because it is so beneficial, aloe vera is an ingredient in hundreds of skin care products. Buy your own aloe vera plant—it'll look beautiful and be an easily accessible remedy for burns!

_____
_____
_____

# EXTRA WRITING PRACTICE

## BEFORE YOU WRITE

*Read the following article. Paraphrase the four underlined sentences using the words provided.*

### The Wonders of Energy Medicine

Of all alternative therapies, energy medicine probably meets with the most skepticism, as remedies are based on invisible powers. Followers believe that healers are able to channel energy into patients through a variety of methods, alleviating their suffering.

*Reiki* was developed by a Japanese Buddhist in 1922. *Rei* and *ki* can be translated as a worldwide power and a vital life force respectively. Combined into one word, it refers to the energy that flows through all living beings and unites them. **1.** Practitioners claim they can transmit this universal spirit to the patient by placing their hands on his or her body. They maintain that this refreshes the spirit and leads to physical wellness.

Crystal healing is a distant approach, which means no healer is present during treatment. Crystals and minerals are used, and they reportedly bring one into a healthy spiritual, mental, and physical state. **2.** According to therapists, these substances regulate the energy patterns within the human body, creating harmony and well-being. Each crystal is said to have a separate set of gifts. To choose a match, one must look at and touch each type of stone. **3.** If a crystal vibrates in the seeker's hands and stirs an inner feeling of peace, he or she will know that is the correct one.

**4.** While many people may be doubtful, some patients who have sought help from traditional medicine with no success have turned to energy medicine in hopes of obtaining relief.

1. _____
   (physical touch, draw power, channel)

2. _____
   (peaceful, healthy, balance)

3. _____
   (shake, calm)

4. _____
   (effective, conventional)

## WRITE IT UP

*Summarize the article above in a 120-word paragraph on a separate piece of paper. Remember to cover the writer's main points using your own words.*

148

## リンガポルタのご案内

> リンガポルタ連動テキストをご購入の学生さんは、
> 「リンガポルタ」を無料でご利用いただけます！

　本テキストで学習していただく内容に準拠した問題を、オンライン学習システム「リンガポルタ」で学習していただくことができます。PCだけでなく、スマートフォンやタブレットでも学習できます。単語や文法、リスニング力などをよりしっかり身に付けていただくため、ぜひ積極的に活用してください。

　リンガポルタの利用にはアカウントとアクセスコードの登録が必要です。登録方法については下記ページにアクセスしてください。

https://www.seibido.co.jp/linguaporta/register.html

本テキスト「New Connection Book 3」のアクセスコードは下記です。

**7181-2050-1231-0365-0003-008b-FVWB-L3LM**

・リンガポルタの学習機能（画像はサンプルです。また、すべてのテキストに以下の4つの機能が用意されているわけではありません）

● 多肢選択

● 空所補充（音声を使っての聞き取り問題も可能）

● 単語並びかえ（マウスや手で単語を移動）

● マッチング（マウスや手で単語を移動）

## TEXT PRODUCTION STAFF

| edited by | 編集 |
| --- | --- |
| Takashi Kudo | 工藤 隆志 |
| Minako Hagiwara | 萩原 美奈子 |

| cover design by | 表紙デザイン |
| --- | --- |
| in-print | インプリント |

| text design by | 本文デザイン |
| --- | --- |
| Ruben Frosali | ルーベン・フロサリ |

## CD PRODUCTION STAFF

| recorded by | 吹き込み者 |
| --- | --- |
| Carolyn Miller (AmE) | キャロリン・ミラー (アメリカ英語) |
| Jack Merluzzi (AmE) | ジャック・マルージ (アメリカ英語) |
| Dominic Allen (AmE) | ドミニク・アレン (アメリカ英語) |
| Rachel Walzer (AmE) | レイチェル・ワルザー (アメリカ英語) |

## New Connection Book 3
### 4技能を高める英語演習 Book 3

2019年1月20日　初版発行
2025年2月10日　第5刷発行

著　　者　角山 照彦
　　　　　Melanie Scooter
　　　　　Courtney Hall

発 行 者　佐野 英一郎

発 行 所　株式会社 成美堂
　　　　　〒101-0052　東京都千代田区神田小川町3-22
　　　　　TEL 03-3291-2261　FAX 03-3293-5490
　　　　　https://www.seibido.co.jp

印刷・製本　(株)加藤文明社

ISBN 978-4-7919-7181-7　　　　　　　　　　　　Printed in Japan

・落丁・乱丁本はお取り替えします。
・本書の無断複写は、著作権上の例外を除き著作権侵害となります。